I0016128

Ubuntu

Server

Version 18.04 LTS

Shiv Kumar Goyal

Preface

Welcome to Ubuntu Server, a quick reference guide for Ubuntu administrators and users. The purpose of writing this book is to help the Ubuntu users in performing day to day tasks on Ubuntu server. The book contains lot of screen shots and output of commands to accomplice the required tasks. This book emphasis on practical aspect of Ubuntu administration therefore you will find procedures with minimal theory. This book covers LVM, ftp, user administration, firewall, NFS, logs and software management etc. I tried to update this book for all new features of Ubuntu 18.04. Hope you will like this book.

Shiv Kumar Goyal

Contents

Chapter 1

Introduction

Linux is an Operating system just like Microsoft Windows and MAC OS. Linux is an open source project started by Linus Torvalds in 1991. Since then Linux has undergone long evolution cycle, from just basic kernel to full fledge Graphical operating system. Today there are thousands of Linux distributions in the market, but most of them are just repackaging of existing Linux distributions. Every day new distributions comes in the market. Every distribution has its own niche of users. Some distributions are specifically made for servers other for desktops, there are many distributions which caters the old hardware machines and some for bleeding edge technologies. The Linux distribution can be classified based on the package system it uses and distribution it is using as its base, for example Centos, Oracle and Scientific Linux is based on Red hat and it uses RPM packaging, Debian based popular distributions are Ubuntu, Mint, Kali Linux, Parsix etc which uses DEB packing. Further distribution can be either free to use or you have to pay for it. The prominent player in free Linux are Ubuntu, Debian, Fedora, Opensuse etc. Redhat and SUSE are major player in non- free enterprise Linux distribution.

Introduction to Ubuntu

Ubuntu is free to use Linux distribution. Canonical Ltd, owned by South African Entrepreneur Mark Shuttleworth, funded Ubuntu project. On 8 July 2005, Mark Shuttleworth and Canonical announced the creation of the Ubuntu Foundation and provided an initial funding of US$10 million. The main aim of the foundation was to provide funds for future development and promotion of Ubuntu Linux.

Ubuntu is Debian based Linux distribution. Ubuntu takes source code from Debian Linux latest unstable branch and adapts them to Ubuntu. Ubuntu also patches and add additional features to these packages if necessary and then push back these enhancements to Debian developer. Ubuntu comes up with new release after every six months. Every forth release is called Long Term Support (LTS) version which is supported with updates and patches up to 5 years. Current LTS version is 18.04 (Code Name **Bionic Beaver**). Ubuntu 18.04 LTS will be supported for 5 years until April 2023. Earlier there were two versions of Ubuntu on Intel platform 32 bit and 64 bit. As all latest hardware available these days are 64 bit therefore Ubuntu has decided to provide only 64 bit image of Ubuntu server. Ubuntu Server is a variant of the standard Ubuntu, tailored for networks and services. It is capable of catering thousands of nodes.

Unlike the installation of Ubuntu Desktop, Ubuntu Server does not include a graphical installation program. Instead, it uses a text menu-based installation process. However, you can add Graphical desktop enviroment later on, if you like working on graphical environment.

What is Debian?

Debian is an organization of volunteers who came together for common cause of developing free software. The Debian is free to use Operating system. The Debian Project was started by Ian Murdock in 1993. The first stable released in 1996. There are more than 51,000 software packages in the Debian repositories, making it the largest software compilation. Debian officially promotes only free software, However you can download and install non free software from the Debian's contrib and non-free repositories.

Ubuntu and Debian

Ubuntu comes up with new release after every six months. Debian has a slightly different policy, they have three branches, stable, testing, and unstable. The Testing and unstable branches comes under development repositories. Unstable and testing branches are updated frequently during the development of the next stable release. All latest packages first arrive in unstable branch (codename "Sid"). Packages from unstable packages are transferred to testing branch when they meet certain criteria. The unstable branch receives new packages as soon as they are uploaded. Every year Debian will freeze the testing branch and prepare it to become the next stable release. New stable release comes after 2 years from the previous one. Total lifetime of new release is about 3 years. The reason behind bringing new Operating system, Ubuntu was long duration between stable releases of Debian. As two years is quite long time in terms of IT industry. Ubuntu uses testing branch of Debian, which has more updated software than its stable branch.

## Chapter 2

New Features in Ubuntu 18.04 LTS

Ubuntu 18.04 has many new features compared to its predecessor versions following are some of the main new features: -

1.   New installer known as **Subiquity** server installer.

2.   Improved UEFI Secure Boot.

3.   Linux Kernel 4.15

4.   OpenJDK

5.   Teaming support in network manager.

6.   **netplan.io** has been replaced with ifupdown

7.   LXD 3.0

8.   QEMU 2.11.1 to fix the spectre/meltdown

9.   libvirt 4.0

10.   Chrony instead of ntpd

11.   Experimental zpool and zfs filesystem support, including ZFS on root

12.   **ubuntu-advantage-tools** including Canonical Livepatch

13.   Apache updated to version 2.4.29

14.   Ubuntu 18.04 includes the latest OpenStack release

## Chapter 3

Minimum System Requirement

Following are minimum requirements to install Ubuntu Linux. However, it is ideal to have more resources than this for optimum working of applications.

Processor   700 MHz or faster

System memory (RAM)   1 GB

Hard disk   10GB

VGA resolution of 1024X 768

Ether **CD/DVD** or **USB** for installer media

Chapter 4

Installation

The installation of Ubuntu server is quite easy. You just have to follow the steps of the installer and provide required input. The common two ways to install: -

1. Automated i.e. Kickstart
2. Interactive

Kickstart

For Kickstart installation, we have to create a single file containing the answers to all the questions installation normally asks during interactive installation. Once the installation starts, no user intervention is required. To generate a Kickstart file, install the **system-config-kickstart** package designed by Redhat. To install this package enable **universe** repository and run **system-config-kickstart**. Kickstart package offers graphical user interface to generate Kickstart file. Place this file on installer's boot media. Pass the parameter to the installer at boot time to tell it to use the file.

Note: Kickstart requires GUI environment installed on system where you prepare this file.

Interactive method

Interactive method is method of installation where user intervention is necessary. Interactive method is normal method used for installation. In the earlier versions of Ubuntu server use to use Ubuntu Installer which is based on Debian Installer. With Ubuntu 18.04 server introduces new installer, the "live server" installer ("subiquity") which provides a more user friendly and faster installation experience. However, you can still use Ubuntu installer for installation. As subiquity is quite new, it has some limitations, which Ubuntu team is trying to solve. Like at time of writing of this book, only supports amd64 processors and does not support LVM or RAID. Installation of Ubuntu is divided in to number of tasks. To perform each task installer asks user necessary questions. Based on the user input installer performs the task accordingly. By default, only essential (high priority) questions will be asked. If you are a power user and like to control each step which is done automatically by the Ubuntu installer, there are two different parameters you can pass at boot time, depending on the how much control you want. For medium level control pass **priority=medium** parameter at boot time and for expert mode you can write **priority=low** at boot time.

The Ubuntu installer for server is text based so mouse will not work. To move forward or backward you have to use

8

keyboard. For moving forward, you can use either **TAB** button or right arrow key. For moving backward use **ALT + TAB** key or left arrow key. The **SPACE BAR** selects an item such as a checkbox. Use **ENTER** key to activate choices. For help press **F1** key. The error messages during installation are logged in **/var/log/syslog**. Once installation is finished these logs are copied to **/var/log/installer/syslog** on your new system.

Dual Boot V/S Single boot

If you are installing Ubuntu server for production environment there will be only one operating system on the server, but if you are, installing Ubuntu server for testing purpose you can install Ubuntu alongside windows operating system. You can setup a dual boot system by installing two operating systems on one drive by partitioning the drive or install both Operating systems on separate hard drives. The Grub bootloader during configuration scans for any other Operating systems installed on your system, regardless of the number of hard drives you have. Once Grub finds additional Operating system, it will add entry for each of them in the Grub boot menu. After installation Grub gives you option to select the operating system to start.

Media preparation

1. To start installation first download media from http://www.ubuntu.com/download/

2. Burn the downloaded ISO image file to DVD.

   Or

   Create USB media with following steps

   1. Download universal USB installer from https://www.pendrivelinux.com/universal-usb-installer-easy-as-1-2-3/

   2. Insert USB media and run the program

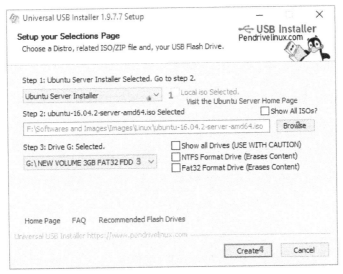

Once USB creation is finished, attach media to machine where you want to do installation.

Steps for installation

1. Change the boot priority in BIOS of the system on which you want to install Ubuntu server and set the installation device you created in the previous section (DVD / USB) as first device. Changing BIOS setting differs from system to system, check the system manual for changing system BIOS setting.

2. Select the language.

3. Keyboard configuration.

4. Select type of Ubuntu installation.

5. Network configuration provides option to use either DHCP provided IP Address or static IP Address. In this step you can will also set name server and gateway.

6. Adding proxy server address for connecting internet if your machine connects to internet using proxy server.

7. Selecting mirror server for Ubuntu updates and additional packages. On this screen, select the mirror that is closest to your location for faster updates.

8. Partitioning the disk. In this step, either you can select the automatic setting or you can manually create partition. Usually in the production environment, you

11

select the manual option. Earlier for Ubuntu to work you require at least two partition, swap and / (root) partition, however in new version you can have only one partition and keep swap as file. However, it is ideal to keep swap as a partition and / and /home partition as separate. The reason for keeping /home partition separate is that in case /home partition is filled 100 % by the user, still the system keeps working. However, if there is /home directory in the root partition instead of separate partition then system will stop working.

9. Create user and password. This user will be used as administrator. For all administration tasks (sudo) this user's password will be used. In this step, you provide name of the system also. This name will be hostname of the system. This hostname should be unique in your network.

10. Select optional features you want to add. These features you can add any time after installation.

11. The system will start copping the files and kernel.

12. After installation, the system will restart and presents you login screen. Use the same username and password you created in the earlier step.

Screen wise installation steps

Once Installation menu comes, Select **Language**

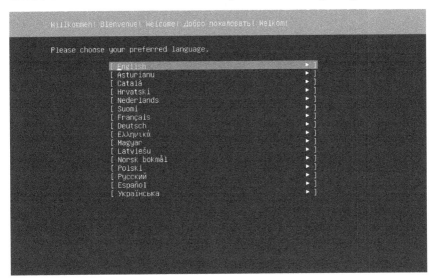

Select **keyboard Language and Keyboard layout**

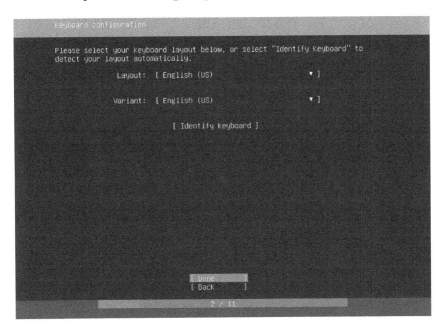

Select **Install Ubuntu**

In the network configuration by default DHCP is selected

For setting up network card with static IP address press spacebar on the network card it will bring options, select **Edit IPv4** option for IPv4 address setting. In the next screen select manual for static IP address.

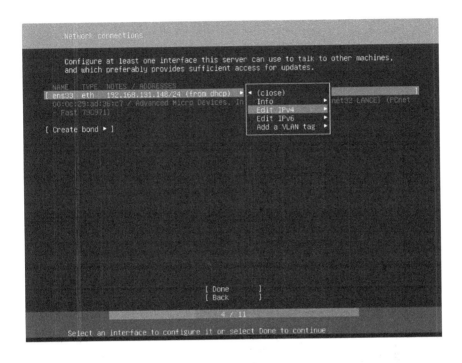

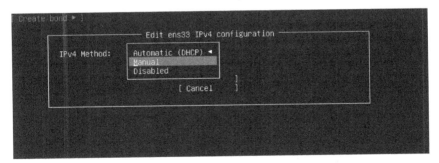

Provide Subnet mask, IP address, Gateway and DNS.

Subnet must be in the CIDR format where network address with subnet should be given.   eg 192.168.1.0/24. Press **Save**.

Provide HTTP proxy address for accessing internet if you don't have any proxy server then keep it blank and press

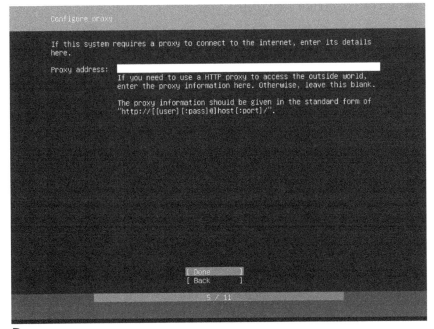

Done.

Select the nearest Ubuntu Mirror for Ubuntu software updates.

Configure Ubuntu archive mirror

If you use an alternative mirror for Ubuntu, enter its details here.

Mirror address: http://archive.ubuntu.com/ubuntu
You may provide an archive mirror that will be used instead of
the default 'http://archive.ubuntu.com/ubuntu'

Now select how to partition the disk. There are three option first **Use An Entire disk**, **Use An Entire disk with LVM** and **Manual** For demonstration purpose we will select **Manual** for custom partitioning (If you want easy installation you can select automatic partition). We will create four partitions / partition 10GB, swap 4GB, /boot 500M and remaining space for /home. For adding partition press spacebar on the disk, in the context menu select **Add Partition.** On the add partition popup windows write **Size** in Megabytes and Gigabytes. For Megabytes add M and G for Gigabytes eg. for 500 MB write 500M and for 2 GB write 2G (Note if you do not specify any size it will take all remaining size). **Format** ext4 for /boot, / and /home and swap for

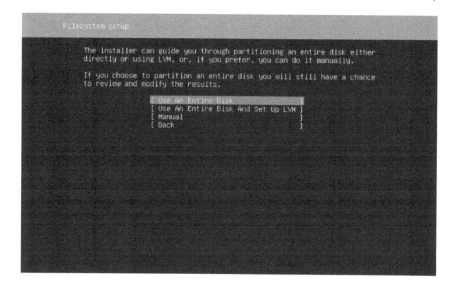

Filesystem setup

The installer can guide you through partitioning an entire disk either
directly or using LVM, or, if you prefer, you can do it manually.

If you choose to partition an entire disk you will still have a chance
to review and modify the results.

[Use An Entire Disk   ]
[Use An Entire Disk And Set Up LVM]
[Manual   ]
[Back   ]

swap partition. **Mount** write mount point except swap. Once finished press done. It will confirm on the next screen

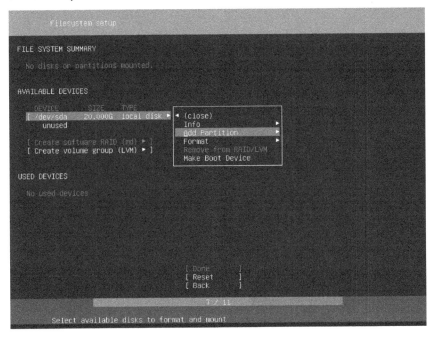

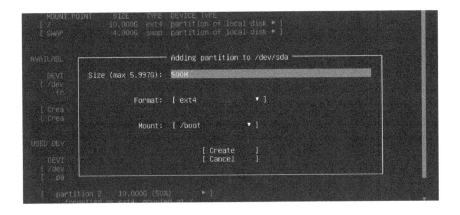

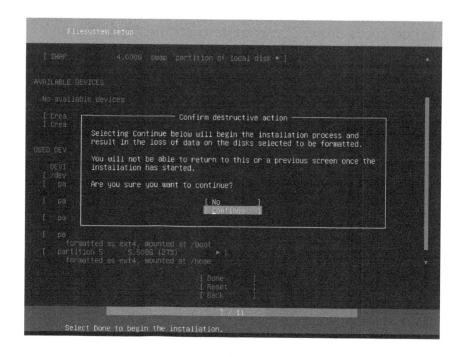

Provide users full name, server name, username and password (This username and password will be used for all

administrator's tasks)

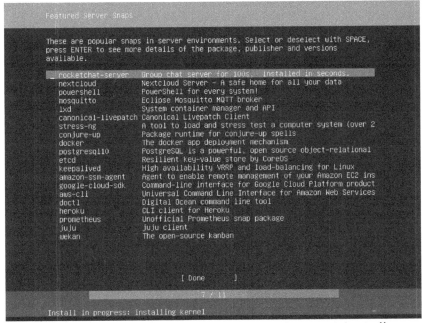

Select the additional components you to want install.

Once system finishes installation, press **Reboot Now.**

22

After reboot you will get Ubuntu login prompt. Login with user you have created during installation.

Connecting MS windows PC to Linux machine

1. Download putty from
   http://www.chiark.greenend.org.uk/~sgtatham/putty/latest.html

2. Install putty on windows PC.

3. After installation start putty.

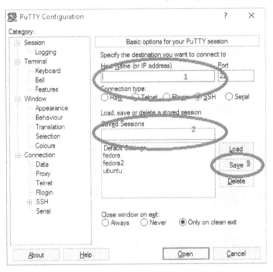

4. Write the IPaddress of the linux machine and give name of session and save.

5. Double click the session name to connect to the Linux Machine.

Sudo and root access

If you are coming from Red hat based Linux, you must have observed during Ubuntu installation you are not prompted for root password creation. **root** is super user or administrator who can do anything on the system. root user has full access on the system. In Ubuntu password created for the first user during installation is used for all administrative tasks. In Ubuntu command **sudo** command issued to do administrator tasks. sudo provides mechanism in which trusted users can do administrative tasks. Sudo approach is more granular, suppose you want a specific user to run only particular administrative command and do not want to give full access of the system, in the conventional Linux you have to share root password, which poses security risk. In case of sudo you do not have to share root password, you can configure the user with sudo and give access to required command only. The user with sudo access have to run this administrative command with preceding sudo word, he will be prompted to enter his own password not the root password. Once authenticated the administrative command is executed and this command will be executed as if it has been run by the root user. By default, the root account itself have login disabled. If you wish, you can enable the root account later by setting a password for it with the command **sudo passwd root**.

Example of sudo command

Chapter 5

Boot process

After pressing power on button to Ubuntu login prompt screen, system do lot of processing to get you to login prompt. This process is known as boot process. It is important to understand the boot process of Linux for configuring Linux and to resolving startup issues.

Boot process of Linux

1. **BIOS**
2. **Master Boot Record**
3. **GRUB 2**

   Uses /boot/grub/grub.cfg to select the kernel image. Do not edit this file. GRUB2 menu-configuration settings uses /etc/default/grub when generating grub.cfg

4. **Kernel**

   1. Mounts the root file system as specified with "root=" in grub.conf
   2. The kernel starts the systemd process with a process ID of 1 (PID 1)
   3. **initrd** stands for Initial RAM Disk. initrd is used by kernel as temporary root file system until kernel is booted and the real root file system is mounted. It also contains drivers, which are required to access hard disk and other necessary hardware.

5. systemd

Systemd is a system and service manager for Linux operating systems. It is designed to be backwards compatible with SysV init scripts, and provides a number of features such as parallel startup of system services at boot time. systemd is the parent process of all processes on a system.

system determine the default system target earlier it used to called as run level. After determining the target, it performs the initialization of system, which includes

1. Setting the host name
2. Initializing the network
3. Initializing the system hardware
4. Mounting the file systems
5. Starting swapping

## Chapter 6

Network

What is computer Network

A computer network is group of computers and computing devices that are linked together. This link provides communication between the different computers and devices in that group. Computer and devices can use wire, fiber optic or microwave as a medium of communication. There are many types of networks but we will focus on TCP/IP as it is most popular suite in use both in Local Area Network (LAN) and Wide Area Network (WAN)) such as internet. In Linux we call each computer as host.

Network basics

Ubuntu Linux is multiuser operating system. As we are discussing Ubuntu server, this may have more than one user connected to this server. The Ubuntu allows you to share the data on the server and also allows you connect multiple users simultaneously to the server. The modern networking protocols uses technique known as packet switching. A packet is small chunk of data with fixed size that is transferred from one computer to other. Packet switching allows single network link to be shared among many computers.

TCPIP

In the Network for all computers and devices to work together, they must use a common protocol, or a set of rules for transmitting and receiving these packets of data. Many protocols have been developed. The International Standards Organization (ISO) developed the Open Systems Interconnection (OSI) model. It divides network communication into seven layers. OSI is a generic, protocol independent standard, acting as a communication gateway between the network and end user. In Modern times one of the most widely used protocol is the Transmission Control Protocol/Internet Protocol (TCP/IP). TCP/IP also is a layered protocol but does not use all of the OSI layers, though the layers are equivalent in operation and function. TCP/IP was developed during the 1960s but was adopted in 1983.

Seven layer of OSI and TCP Mapping

OSI Model	TCP Model	Application	Address	Devices
7:Application layer	Application Layer	HTTP / Telnet / SSH	Applications DNS, DHCP. ntp, HTTP	
6:Presentation layer		SSL / MIME		
5:Session layer		Sockets and Remote Procedure Call (RPC)		
4: Transport layer	Transport layer	Transmission Control Protocol (TCP)	TCP/UDP	Gateway
3: Network layer	Internet layer	Internet Protocol (IP)	IP4, IP6, IPX, ICMP	Router, firewall Layer 3 switch
2: Data link layer	Network Access Layer	Ethernet / Frame Relay	MAC address, ARP	Bridge Layer 2 switch
1: Physical layer		IEEE 802.x	Ethernet	HUB

TCP/IP uses many hardware, the most common type is Ethernet. These days Ethernet can be of different speed like Megabytes and Gigabytes. You require network card on computer to connect to the network. An Ethernet card is one kind of network adapter. These adapters support the Ethernet standard for high-speed network connections. Every network card has physical address known as Media Access control address (MAC address). MAC address works on layer

2 of OSI model. Manufacturer of network interface card assigns MAC addresses. To access the network card, we assign IP address to network card, which works on layer 3 of OSI model. Hosts on different network can connect using layer3. As IP address are still numeric value it is difficult to remember more over there is possibility of IP address may change over the time. To make life easy we use name of host known as **hostname**.

Ubuntu server comes with a number of graphical utilities to configure your network devices. As a server administrator you should focus more on managing your network through command line. This book will teach you how to accomplish common network administration task on command line.

Ethernet interface

Ethernet interfaces are identified as device name string starting with **en** it can be eno1 , ens33 or any name.

Identify Ethernet interfaces

To check the all available Ethernet interfaces you can issue **ip** command with **a** option

```
adams@server1:~$ ip a
1: lo: <LOOPBACK,UP,LOWER_UP> mtu 65536 qdisc noqueue state UNKNOWN
group default qlen 1000
    link/loopback 00:00:00:00:00:00 brd 00:00:00:00:00:00
    inet 127.0.0.1/8 scope host lo
       valid_lft forever preferred_lft forever
```

```
    inet6 ::1/128 scope host
       valid_lft forever preferred_lft forever
2: ens33: <BROADCAST,MULTICAST,UP,LOWER_UP> mtu 1500 qdisc fq_codel
state UNKNOWN group default qlen 1000
    link/ether 00:0c:29:ad:36:c7 brd ff:ff:ff:ff:ff:ff
    inet 192.168.131.149/24 brd 192.168.131.255 scope global dynamic
ens33
       valid_lft 968sec preferred_lft 968sec
    inet6 fe80::20c:29ff:fead:36c7/64 scope link
       valid_lft forever preferred_lft forever
```
This command shows two adapters first is Loop back adapter and other
is physical adapter.

First adapter in this command output is **lo** which is loopback
adapter. Loopback adapter is virtual adapter which is not tied
to any physical adapter. loopback adapter enables testing of
the IP stack. In some instances, it is used for process to
process communication on same machine.

Query hardware information of Ethernet interface

For quickly checking hardware information of all network
interface and their device name **lshw** command can be used.
lshw command should be used with **sudo** as it is
administrator command.

```
adams@server1:~$ sudo lshw -class network
[sudo] password for adams:
  *-network
       description: Ethernet interface
       product: 79c970 [PCnet32 LANCE]
       vendor: Advanced Micro Devices, Inc. [AMD]
```

32

```
physical id: 1
bus info: pci@0000:02:01.0
logical name: ens33
version: 10
serial: 00:0c:29:ad:36:c7
size: 10Mbit/s
width: 32 bits
clock: 33MHz
capabilities: bus_master rom ethernet physical logical tp aui
configuration: autonegotiation=off broadcast=yes
driver=pcnet32 driverversion=1.35 duplex=half ip=192.168.131.149
latency=64 link=yes maxlatency=255 mingnt=6 multicast=yes
port=twisted pair speed=10Mbit/s
resources: irq:19 ioport:2000(size=128) memory:fd500000-
fd50ffff
```

Change or query parameters of Ethernet interface

ethtool command with interface name is used to query or change the hardware parameters of the Ethernet interface like speed, wake-on-lan, duplex mode and auto negotiation. This command should be used with sudo.

Query

adams@server1:~$ **sudo ethtool ens33**
```
Settings for ens33:
        Supported ports: [ TP AUI ]
        Supported link modes:   Not reported
        Supported pause frame use: No
        Supports auto-negotiation: No
        Supported FEC modes: Not reported
        Advertised link modes:  Not reported
        Advertised pause frame use: No
```

33

```
    Advertised auto-negotiation: No
    Advertised FEC modes: Not reported
    Speed: 10Mb/s
    Duplex: Half
    Port: Twisted Pair
    PHYAD: 0
    Transceiver: internal
    Auto-negotiation: off
    MDI-X: Unknown
    Current message level: 0x00000007 (7)
                           drv probe link
    Link detected: yes
```

Change the configuration

```
~$ sudo ethtool --change ens33 speed 100 duplex full
[sudo] password for adams:
adams@server1:~$
```

Note If you have made any change using the **ethtool**, these changes are not persistent and get lost after reboot. To make these changes permanent you have specify these command in startup scripts.

IP address

In this section we will discuss how to discover the IP Address of running Ubuntu server. First thing is to query IP address assigned to all network card. If you want to show the IP Address of specific adapter you can add the adapter name.

Show IP address

```
ip addr show
```

Or

```
ifconfig -a
```

To see the IP Address of specific adapter

```
adams@server1:~$ ip addr show ens33
2: ens33: <BROADCAST,MULTICAST,UP,LOWER_UP> mtu 1500 qdisc
fq_codel state UNKNOWN group default qlen 1000
    link/ether 00:0c:29:ad:36:c7 brd ff:ff:ff:ff:ff:ff
    inet 192.168.131.149/24 brd 192.168.131.255 scope global
dynamic ens33
        valid_lft 922sec preferred_lft 922sec
    inet6 fe80::20c:29ff:fead:36c7/64 scope link
        valid_lft forever preferred_lft forever
```

This command shows IP Address in the format 192.168.131.149/24. Here 192.168.131.149 is the IP Address assigned to network interface 24 is Netmask. An IP address is composed of 32 bits. These 32 bits is divided in two parts network address and the host address. The net mask defines how many bits are used for network i.e. /24 or 255.255.255.0, these are two ways of saying that the network address starts 24 bits from the left i.e. 192.168.131 and remaining bits are for host. In this example last octet is for host. The Netmask defines how many hosts can be there in the network.

Standard Netmask

Class	Number of hosts	Netmask Length	Netmask
Class A	16,777,214	8	255.0.0.0
Class B	65,534	16	255.255.0.0
Class C	254	24	255.255.255.0

Show Link status

```
ip link show
```

Show routing table and default gateway

When you want to connect to IP Address which is of different range than your own network then you require gateway to connect to that IP Address. Gateway routes the traffic to the different IP. Default gateway is address of the device which routes the traffic to different network incase system not able to reach to the destination address. When you know the route to the destination you can specify route explicitly. Show the routing table **ip route** command can be used

```
adams@server1:~$ ip route
default via 192.168.131.2 dev ens33 proto dhcp src 192.168.131.153
metric 100
192.168.131.0/24 dev ens33 proto kernel scope link src
192.168.131.153
192.168.131.2 dev ens33 proto dhcp scope link src 192.168.131.153
metric 100
```

Or

```
netstat -rn
```

Show Link status

Syntax

```
ip link show
```

Example

```
adams@server1:~$ ip link show
1: lo: <LOOPBACK,UP,LOWER_UP> mtu 65536 qdisc noqueue state
UNKNOWN mode DEFAULT group default qlen 1000
    link/loopback 00:00:00:00:00:00 brd 00:00:00:00:00:00
2: ens33: <BROADCAST,MULTICAST,UP,LOWER_UP> mtu 1500 qdisc
fq_codel state UP mode DEFAULT group default qlen 1000
    link/ether 00:0c:29:c3:30:c6 brd ff:ff:ff:ff:ff:ff
```

Assign the IP Address temporarily

In this section we will learn how to assign the IP address to interface temporarily. The command we will give to assign IP Address will take effect immediately but the changes will not be persistent and will lost after reboot.

Syntax

```
ip addr add ip_address dev device_name
```

Example

37

```
$ sudo ip addr add 10.10.10.122/24 dev ens33
```

Check the newly assigned IP Address

```
$ ip addr show ens33
```

Temporary assign/change the default gateway

Syntax

```
ip route add default via gateway_address
```

Example

```
$ sudo ip route add default via 192.168.131.1
```

To verify the default gateway

```
$ ip route show
```

To set link status you can use

```
$ ip link set dev ens33 up
```

To bring down the link to the adapter

```
$ ip link set dev ens33 down
```

Netplan

The way Ubuntu manages network interfaces has completely changed in Ubuntu 18.04. Netplan is a new utility introduced by Ubuntu recently. It the part of Ubuntu server 18.04. This new tool replaces the static interfaces (/etc/network/interfaces) file that had previously been used to configure Ubuntu network interfaces. Netplan is utility for easily configuring networking on Ubuntu system. Netplan reads YAML network configuration files under directory /etc/netplan/. Netplan will generate all the necessary configuration files for chosen renderer tool. Currently two renderer tools are supported by Netplan.

1. NetworkManager
2. Systemd-network

NetworkManager and systemd-network are the system daemon which manages network configuration. Ubuntu server uses systemd-network render.

Assigning static IP address (permanent)

In the earlier section, we have learned how to assign IP address, but that IP Address will not persist after reboot. To assign IP address which stays after reboot. You have to create netplan configuration in the file **/etc/netplan/99_config.yaml**. In the example below we will assign IP Address, Netmask, Gateway and Name server to ens33 Ethernet interface. Edit the file with vi or any other editor. Write down the IP Address, Gateway and name server as shown in this sample file: -

```
network:
    version: 2
    ethernets:
```

```
ens33:
    addresses: [192.168.131.140/24]
    gateway4: 192.168.131.2
    nameservers:
      addresses: [8.8.8.8,8.8.4.4]
```

Once ready apply changes with:

```
$ sudo netplan apply
```

In case you face some issues

```
$ sudo netplan --debug apply
```

Dynamic IP Address Assignment

In last section we configured static IP address of server using Netplan. In this section we will configure our server to use DHCP Server for IP Address assignment. When we configure our machine as DHCP client the IP addresses are assigned dynamically by the DHCP server. First we will create a Netplan configuration in the file /etc/netplan/99_config.yaml. In the example below assumes that you are configuring Ethernet interface identified as ens33.

```
network:
    ethernets:
        ens33:
            addresses: []
            dhcp4: true
    version: 2
```

Apply changes with

```
$ sudo netplan apply
```

In case you face some issues

```
$ sudo netplan --debug apply
```

Check and change hostname

Query hostname

```
hostname
```

Change hostname

Whenever you want to change hostname, you have to change in two steps

1. Change the hostname using command **hostnamectl**
2. Change it in **/etc/hosts**

Use hostnamectl or hostname command to query the current hostname

```
user1@server1:~$ hostnamectl
      Static hostname: server1
            Icon name: computer-vm
              Chassis: vm
           Machine ID: 1b7b53c91c277b88c4b8691e58e4e5fe
              Boot ID: 3d970d5b853f4257ba169ae5927db14f
       Virtualization: vmware
     Operating System: Ubuntu 16.04.2 LTS
               Kernel: Linux 4.4.0-62-generic
```

```
Architecture: x86-64
```

Or

```
Hostname
```

Change the hostname

Syntax

```
hostnamectl set-hostname new_host_name
```

Example

```
$ sudo hostnamectl set-hostname server2
```

1. Next step is to change **/etc/hosts** file

```
127.0.0.1    server2 localhost.localdomain localhost
```

Name Resolution

Whenever you write hostname instead of IP address to ping or to connect Linux host, you have multiple option to resolve hostname to IP address.

- Local file i.e./etc/hosts
- DNS server
- NIS

/etc/hosts

Using local file **/etc/hosts** for hostname to IP address mapping provides ability to store list of hostname to their respective IP address you don't require to look for DNS server. It is very useful if you are connecting to limited servers due scope or security reason you do not have to depend on DNS server.

Format

```
IP_address     hostname aliases
```

Example

```
127.0.0.1                   server1localhost
::1                         server1 localhost
```

Using DNS

/etc/resolv.conf

Traditionally, the file /etc/resolv.conf was a static configuration file DNS server IP address. But with use netplan this has been changed Systemd-resolved handles name server configuration. Now /etc/resolv.conf file just symbolic link to **/run/systemd/resolve/stub-resolv.conf** So if you want to give address of resolver DNS server give it in **/etc/netplan/99_config.yaml** file under respective interface. You can have multiple DNS in this file.

```
network:
    version: 2
    ethernets:
      ens33:
        addresses: [192.168.131.140/24]
```

```
gateway4: 192.168.131.2
nameservers:
    addresses: [8.8.8.8,8.8.4.4]
```

Changing order for hostname resolution

/etc/nsswitch.conf

Suppose your system is configured as DNS client and also as NIS client, whenever you do hostname resolution the system first looks for local file (**/etc/hosts**) for entry of hostname and respective IP address. If there is no entry, it use DNS for resolution it DNS server fails to resolve then it will check it on NIS. However, you can change the priority in which services server uses for hostname resolution by changing /etc/nsswitch.conf

```
vi /etc/nsswitch.conf
```

```
#hosts:        db files nisplus nis dns
hosts:         files dns
```

In this example search sequence is first files means **/etc/hosts** then DNS server.

Important Network Commands

Task	Command
Check connectivity between two system	ping IP Address Example ping 10.1.1.2
Check IP address configuration	ifconfig –a or ip addr show
Check routing table	ip route show netstat –rn
Querying Domain Name System	dig
Local file to resolve hosts to IP address	/etc/hosts
DNS server configuration file	/etc/Netplan/*.yaml
Arp is used to translate IP addresses into MAC addresses	arp
Makes queries to the DNS server to translate IP to a name, or vice versa	nslookup <ipaddress>/<Hostname>
Trace the route of IP packets	traceroute
Query or change the hardware parameters of the Ethernet interface	ethtool

## Chapter 7

Users and Groups

As Linux is a multi-user operating system, it allows multiple users on different computers to access a single system. As a system administrator you required to perform users and group management. The user administration includes addition, modification and removal of users and groups. The user management is critical part of system administration. Improper users and groups leads to compromised system.

Users

A **user** is anyone who uses a computer. Users on a Linux machine is ether people or accounts. Some system services also run using restricted or privileged user accounts.

UID

Linux assign unique user id to every user exist on system which in known as UID or User ID. UID for root user is always 0. For regular user, User ID starts from 1000. Whenever you add new user next available number is assigned to the new user.

User	UID
root	0
System users	1 – 999
Regular users	1000 +

Groups

Users are further logically grouped together in **groups**. Group is logical entity to organize users together based on their properties. It can be either same department, same place or same work.

Every user we create belongs to group and all groups have group ID. List of all available groups can be found in /etc/group and entry of all users who are member of these groups.

There are two type of groups: -

- primary group
- secondary group

Primary group

This is the group applied to your login and used by default when you create new files and directories. It is normally same name as username. When you create new user using adduser command this group automatically get created and the new user will be member of this group. Users primary group ID is written in **/etc/passwd** file for respective users in the third field.

Secondary/ Supplementary Group

These are the groups users are member other than primary group

/etc/group

```
groupname:shadow password:GID:list of users in group
```

Example

```
science:x:1003:class1, class2
```

Changing primary group

```
$ sudo usermod -g data1 user1
```

Changing secondary group

```
$ sudo usermod -G data2 user1
```

Add new group

```
$ sudo groupadd groupname
```

Delete group

```
$ sudo groupdel groupname
```

/etc/passwd

Stores user information

Format

```
username:x:UID:GID:Full_user_name:home_directory:shellaccount
```

Username up to 8 characters. Case-sensitive

x   Passwords are stored in the ``/etc/shadow'' file.

UID   User ID

GID   Group ID

shell account   Often set to **/bin/bash** to provide access to the bash shell but can be other shell like c shell, korn shell etc

Example

```
user1:x:1000:1000:user1,,,:/home/user1:/bin/bash
```

/etc/shadow

Stores actual password in encrypted format

Format

```
username:password:last_password_change:minimum
```

Explanation

Username

up to 8 characters. Case-sensitive, usually all lowercase. A direct match to the username in the /etc/passwd file.

Password

13 character encrypted. A blank entry (eg. ::) indicates a password is not required to log in (usually a bad idea), and a * entry (eg. :*:) indicates the account has been disabled.

last_password_change

The number of days (since January 1, 1970) since the password was last changed.

Minimum

The number of days before password may be changed (0 indicates it may be changed at any time).

Maximum

The number of days after which password must be changed (99999 indicates user can keep his or her password unchanged for many, many years).

Warn

The number of days to warn user of an expiring password (7 for a full week).

Inactive

The number of days after password expires that account is disabled.

Expire

The number of days since January 1, 1970 that an account has been disabled.

Example

```
user1:$6$0USeZ0gR$y.lhVjpu6epAlir1:17261:0:99999:7:::
```

Normal user v/s super user

The superuser (root) is special user who has complete access to the operating system and its configuration. The superuser or administrator user is intended for administrative use only. In traditional Unix systems there use to be **root** user for doing administrative task. Root user has unlimited privileges. Root can access any file, run any program, execute any system call, and modify any setting.

Conventionally with Unix based system, if you wanted to perform administrative tasks, you had to login as root or with the su command ("su" is short form for superuser.). The drawback of using root users is that you have very less control over it and you cannot provide partial access. However, in Ubuntu there is concept of **sudo**, it is used in place of root. The root account is disabled is Ubuntu. This is because the root password is not set in Ubuntu. Sudo allows users and groups access to commands they normally would not be able to use. Sudo provides more granular and flexible approach toward system administration. Sudo will allow a user to have administration privileges without logging in as root. The two best advantages about using sudo command are:

- Restricted privileges
- Logs of the actions taken by users

In order to provide a user with sudo ability, their name should be added to the **sudoers** file. This file is very critical

52

to system and therefore should not be edited directly with a text editor. If the sudoers file is edited incorrectly, it could result in preventing access to the system. Therefore, Ubuntu provides **visudo** command to edit the sudoers file.

To edit this file, first log into your system as user which was created during installation. Give the command **sudo visudo** and provide the password. It will open the sudoers file which is located at /etc/ directory.

Below is the portion of the sudoers file that shows the users with sudo access

adams@server1:~$ **sudo cat /etc/sudoers**

```
Defaults        env_reset
Defaults        mail_badpass
Defaults
secure_path="/usr/local/sbin:/usr/local/bin:/usr/sbin:/usr/bin
:/sbin:/bin:/snap/bin"


# Host alias specification

# User alias specification
# Cmnd alias specification
# User privilege specification
root    ALL=(ALL:ALL) ALL
# Members of the admin group may gain root privileges
%admin ALL=(ALL) ALL
# Allow members of group sudo to execute any command
%sudo   ALL=(ALL:ALL) ALL
# See sudoers(5) for more information on "#include"
directives:
```

```
#includedir /etc/sudoers.d
```

Enable root user

As mentioned by default you will not be able to login as root user as it is in case of other Linux distros. This does not mean root user is not there, it is present but its password is not set. If situation arises in which you require direct root login. Below is the procedure to that.

```
$ sudo passwd
```

It will ask your password provide the password

Now it will ask password you want keep for root

```
adams@server1:~$ sudo passwd
[sudo] password for adams:
Enter new UNIX password:
Retype new UNIX password:
passwd: password updated successfully
```

Now you will able login as root user on the server.

Enable SSH root login

After setting root password which we have done in previous section, you will be able to login on the server itself. However, you will not be able login as root if you try to do at ssh client which is connected to server using ssh connection using putty or other ssh client. To enable root access on ssh you have to change ssh server configuration file. Open and edit **/etc/ssh/sshd_config** and change line

```
#PermitRootLogin prohibit-password
```

To

```
PermitRootLogin yes
```

After that, restart the sshd service

```
# sudo service ssh restart
```

Try login as root on the remote terminal

```
login as: root
root@192.168.131.140's password:
Welcome to Ubuntu 18.04.1 LTS (GNU/Linux 4.15.0-33-generic
x86_64)
root@server1:~#
```

User management

The process of user management which includes adding modifying and deleting user is very simple and straight forward.

Add User

To add new user to Ubuntu you can use **adduser** command. It is interactive command which uses useradd command in the backend. When you issue adduser command it will prompt for initial password which want to set for this user (User can change password once he or she login). It will also ask its full name and other information. The adduser command creates group with same name as of user which will be its primary group. It also create folder in the /home directory.

Syntax

```
$sudo adduser username
```

Example

```
adams@server1:~$ sudo adduser user2
[sudo] password for adams:
Adding user `user2' ...
Adding new group `user2' (1001) ...
Adding new user `user2' (1001) with group `user2' ...
Creating home directory `/home/user2' ...
Copying files from `/etc/skel' ...
Enter new UNIX password:
Retype new UNIX password:
passwd: password updated successfully
Changing the user information for user2
Enter the new value, or press ENTER for the default
        Full Name []: user2
        Room Number []:
        Work Phone []:
        Home Phone []:
        Other []:
Is the information correct? [Y/n] Y
```

Delete user

deluser command is used in Ubuntu to delete the user and its primary group which was created when we have used adduser command. This command will not delete its home directory. It is up to you to delete or retain the directory according to your requirement and company policy.

Syntax:

```
sudo deluser username
```

adams@server1:~$ **sudo deluser user2**

Removing user `user2' ...

Warning: group `user2' has no more members.

Done.

Modify user

Adduser command is for creating user, if you want to change the attributes of the existing user then you have to use usermod command. Following are the few main options you can use with usermod command to modify the user attributes, for more options check man pages of usermod command.

-g   Change the primary group

-G   Change the secondary/supplementary group

-d   Change home directory

-L   Lock user

-U   Unlock the user

-e   Change expire date of the user

-l   Change login name

Syntax

usermod [options] username

Example

Lock user using usermod command

```
$ sudo usermod -L user1
```

Unlock user using usermod command

```
$ sudo usermod –U user1
```

Change Full name (Comment)

```
$sudo usermod -c "database user" username
```

Password

Although Ubuntu is very secure by design, there are many reasons for the security breach. It can be either user ignorance or user carelessness. However, one of the main reason is weak passwords. As a System administrator, you should make policy in your organization that user must adhere to strong password. This can be done forcing minimum password length, complexity level and maximum password lifetime.

First look in to some basic commands for password management.

Change own password

```
$ passwd
```

Changing password for other user (If you have access)

Syntax

```
sudo passwd username
```

Example

```
$ sudo passwd user1
```

List password expiry information of the user

Syntax

```
sudo chage -l username
```

Example

```
adams@server1:~$ sudo chage -l user1
Last password change                              : Sep 07, 2018
Password expires                                  : Oct 07, 2018
Password inactive                                 : never
Account expires                                   : never
Minimum number of days between password change       : 0
Maximum number of days between password change       : 30
Number of days of warning before password expires    : 7
```

Interactive command for changing password expirations

Syntax

```
$ sudo chage username
```

Example

adams@server1:~$ **sudo chage user1**

Changing the aging information for user1

Enter the new value, or press ENTER for the default

     Minimum Password Age [0]:

     Maximum Password Age [99999]: 30

     Last Password Change (YYYY-MM-DD) [2018-09-07]:

     Password Expiration Warning [7]:

     Password Inactive [-1]:

     Account Expiration Date (YYYY-MM-DD) [-1]:

Force user to change password at next login

$ sudo chage -d 0 user1

Change minimum length

You can use PAM (Pluggable Authentication Module) to enforce password complexity. By default, Ubuntu's minimum password length is 6. Suppose you would like to change the minimum length to 8 characters. To change the minimum length of password to 8 characters add **minlen=8** after following line in **/etc/pam.d/common-password** file

password [success=1 default=ignore] pam_unix.so obscure sha512

Modified line looks like that

password [success=1 default=ignore] pam_unix.so obscure sha512 minlen=8

Display information about user

Show current user information

```
$id
```

Show users information for other user

```
$ sudo id username
```

## Chapter 8

Process and threads

Every task done by Linux OS has process associated with it. Processes have following properties: -

- Process has priority based on the context switches on them.
- Each process provide required resources to execute the program.
- Each process starts with single thread known as primary thread.
- Process can have multiple threads.

Process runs in foreground and background

Foreground Processes

A foreground process is any command or task you run directly and wait for it to complete.

Background Process

Background process are process which runs behind the scene. Unlike with a foreground process, the shell does not have to wait for a background process to end before it can run more processes. The maximum number of process that can run in background depends on amount of memory available.

Commands

Command	Description
bg	Sends job to Background
fg	Bring job to foreground
jobs	Show current jobs
kill	Stops the process
ps	Show the process information
&	if command ends with the & the shell execute the command in background and shell will not wait for finish Example gcalctool &

Bring command to foreground

```
$ fg
ctrl + c
```

Check the running jobs

```
$ jobs
```

List the current running process

```
$ ps –ef
```

or

```
$ ps aux
```

Kill the process forcefully

First check the process ID with `ps -ef` command then

```
$ sudo kill -9 <process -id >
```

Monitoring the process with ps command

ps command show the percentage of CPU & memory utilization of the process it is very useful if your machine is under performing. **ps** command gives you indication which process is hogging memory/CPU.

Process scheduling

Scheduler is part of kernel, which select process to run next. The purpose is to run the processes according to priorities. To set the priority of running process **nice** and **renice** command is used which decide how longer or smaller CPU time is given to process.

Nice   set the priority or niceness of new process.

renice   adjust nice value of running process

niceness of -20 is highest priority and 19 is lowest priority. The default priority is 0

Example

```
$ sudo nice -n 19 cp -r /as /map
```

Commands show priorities of running processes

```
ps -al
```

or

```
top
```

To change the priority

```
$ sudo renice -n 10 <pid>
```

Note: You need root/superuser privilege to change to higher priority.

## Chapter 9

Automating tasks

Linux has utilities to automate the task which system administrator do regularly or at specified time. Following are the main utilities

- Cron
- Anacron
- at

Cron

cron is daemon that can be used to schedule the execution of recurring tasks according to time, day of month, day of week. It accepts machine to be running continuously like server usually do. If at the time of schedule, the system is down it will skip the task.

Configuration file

/etc/crontab

Command

Command	Description
crontab –l	List crontab entries
crontab –e	Edit crontab
crontab –r	Remove crontab

Format

minutes hours Day_of_month Month Day_of_week   Command

Where

Minutes	(from 0 to 59)
hours	(from 0 to 23)
day of month	(from 1 to 31)
month	(from 1 to 12)
day of week	(from 0 to 6) (0=Sunday)

To schedule a recurring task

1. Edit crontab by giving command **crontab –e**

2. Add entries at bottom of file press **i**

Suppose you want to run backup script every night at 11:30

23 * * *   /myscripts/backup.sh

3. Press **ESCAPE** key and press **:** write **x** after that press **ENTER** to save the entry.

Anacron

Anacorn is also to execute the scheduled tasks, unlike cron it is meant for laptop and pc users where machine is not up 24x7. Anacron remembers the scheduled jobs if the system is not running at the time when the job is scheduled. The job is then executed as soon as the system is up. However, Anacron can only run a job once a day. Just like how cron has **/etc/crontab**, anacron has **/etc/anacrontab**.

Anacrontab file format.

```
period    delay    job-identifier    command
```

at

crontab is used for periodic task but for one time tasks at specified time **at** and **batch** commands are used.

To start process at 4 o'clock

```
$ at 4:00
at >ls
ctrl + d
```

Display list of pending jobs

```
atq
```

## Chapter 10

Log management

Log files are very useful in troubleshooting and auditing system for unauthorized system access. Log files give you idea what system was doing at specific point in time. Suppose your machine is running slow or not working properly as a Linux administrator first thing to look for problem is logs. Logs provides an idea when and what problem started and what part of OS is giving problem. Because most of the applications in OS keeps logs. **Rsyslog** and **Journal**, the two logging applications present on the system, have several distinguishing features that make them suitable for specific use cases. In many situations, it is useful to combine their capabilities.

Rsyslogd

Some logs are controlled by rsyslogd daemon. It is enhanced replacement of **sysklogd**. It offers high-performance, great security features, modular design and support for transportation via the TCP or UDP protocols. Every logged message contains at least a time and normally a program name field.

/etc/rsyslog.conf

The rsyslog.conf file is the main configuration file for the rsyslogd which logs system messages on the systems. This file specifies rules for logging rsyslogd. List of log files maintained by **rsyslogd** can be found in the rsyslog.conf configuration file. Log files are usually located in the /var/log/ directory.

Sample rsyslog.conf

```
etc]$ cat rsyslog.conf
# rsyslog v5 configuration file

# For more information see /usr/share/doc/rsyslog-*/rsyslog_conf.html
# If you experience problems, see
http://www.rsyslog.com/doc/troubleshoot.html

*.info;mail.none;authpriv.none;cron.none
/var/log/messages

# The authpriv file has restricted access.
authpriv.*                                              /var/log/secure

# Log all the mail messages in one place.
mail.*                                                  -
/var/log/maillog


# Log cron stuff
cron.*                                                  /var/log/cron

# Everybody gets emergency messages
*.emerg                                                 *
```

70

```
# Save news errors of level crit and higher in a special file.
uucp,news.crit
/var/log/spooler

# Save boot messages also to boot.log
local7.*
/var/log/boot.log
```

Log filtering with rsyslog.conf

There is too much logging happens in the system, if it is not filtered it become almost impossible to use these logs. To filter the logs, we use **/etc/rsyslog.conf** file. It has two parameter facility and priority separated with dot(.). **Facility** is name of process for which you want to log and **priority** specify level of log like **debug**, **info**, **notice**, **warning**, **err**, **crit**, **alert**, **emerg** or * for all type of messages you want to keep.

Example

```
# The authpriv file has restricted access.
authpriv.*
/var/log/secure

# Log all the mail messages in one place.
mail.*                                         -
/var/log/maillog
```

In the example where **authpriv** and **mail** is facility and **priority** is * which means all logs.

71

journald

Logs can also be managed by the **journald** daemon – a component of systemd. It's a centralized location for all messages logged by different components in a systemd enabled Linux system. This includes kernel and boot messages, initial RAM disk, messages coming from syslog or different services, it indexes and makes them available to the user. Log data collected by the journal is primarily text-based but can also include binary data where necessary. Log files produced by journald are not persistent, log files are stored only in memory or a small ring-buffer in the **/run/log/journal/** directory. The amount of logged data depends on free memory. Logs gets rotated periodically. But you can configure the system to make these logs persistent.

Viewing log with journalctl

To view log

```
journalctl
```

To view full meta data about all entries

```
journalctl -o verbose
```

Live view of logs

```
journalctl -f
```

Filtering by Priority

You can filter the logs on basis of priority.

Syntax

```
journalctl -p priority
```

Example

In this example we want to view only lines with error from the log

```
journalctl -p err
```

To view log entries only from the current boot

```
journalctl -b
```

To make logs persistent

```
$ sudo mkdir -p /var/log/journal
```

Then, restart journald to apply the change:

```
systemctl restart systemd-journald
```

Rotating logs with logrotate

Logs needs rotation to avoid filling of file systems and make log more manageable. Once log file is rotated, it will be renamed with new file name. After certain time of rotation, older log files gets deleted to save space.

logrotate package manages automatic rotation of log files according to configuration in **/etc/logrotate.conf** or otherwise specified with command option

Install

```
sudo apt install logrotate
```

To verify if logrotate installed successfully

```
logrotate
```

Some of the important configuration settings in /etc/logrotate.conf file are rotation-interval, log-file-size, permssions of files, missingok, rotation-count and compression.

Example

```
/var/log/dpkg.log {
    missingok
    monthly
    compress
    rotate 15
size 100M
}
```

In this example the log rotation utility rotate the logs of dpkg with following details :-

Missingok   ignore if logs are missing

Compress   compress the logs in gzip format

Monthly   log is rotated on monthly.

rotate 15   15 days of logs would be kept.

Size 100M   if logs become size of 100 megabytes it will be rotated otherwise it will be rotated at rotation interval i.e. monthly

Monitor logs with logwatch

Logwatch is log monitoring utility. It analyzes and reports short digest of logs of services you wish via mail. Can be configured with configuration file **/usr/share/logwatch/default.conf/logwatch.conf**.

To Install logwatch

```
sudo apt install logwatch
```

Configuration File

/usr/share/logwatch/default.conf/logwatch.conf.

Example

```
# Default person to mail reports to.  Can be a local account or a
# complete email address.  Variable Print should be set to No to
# enable mail feature.
MailTo = root
Service = sendmail
Service = http
Service = sudo
```

In this sample file there two things which are interesting, first the mail address to whom daily digest (report) are sent **mailto = root** in this case root.

76

Second you will receive reports of specific services in this case **sendmail, http and sudo** otherwise you can also write **Service = All** if you want report of all services.

Chapter 11

Software management

Ubuntu package uses comprehensive package management system. It is based on Debian package system. Debian packages have extension of .deb. and exists in repositories. Where repository is warehouse of software collection. It can be either locally like DVDROM, directory or remotely like HTTP, FTP site. Packages contained in repository are precompiled binary format. It is far easier to install packages than installing from source files, which require compiling. With source packages there is another problem of dependencies, as package you are installing may require some libraries or other binaries to be there to function properly. Ubuntu package management system is sophisticated enough to resolve dependencies itself. Several tools are available for using Ubuntu package management system.

APT Advance package tool

APT (Advanced Package Tool) is a one of the tool for managing packages on Debian based distributions. apt provides a high level command line interface for the package management system. **apt** can be used to:

- Install packages
- Remove packages
- Update packages
- Search packages

Install package

Syntax

```
$ sudo apt install package_name
```

Example

```
$ sudo apt install zip
```

Remove package

Syntax

```
$ sudo apt remove package_name
```

Example

```
$ sudo apt remove zip
```

Remove package and its configuration files also

apt remove command removes the package but keeps its configuration files. To remove package completely use **purge** command

Syntax

```
$ sudo apt purge package_name
```

Example

```
$ sudo apt purge zip
```

Update the Package Index

Update command is used for downloading package information from all configured sources. This information is used by other apt commands.

```
$ sudo apt update
```

Upgrade the packages to latest from the repository

Upgrade option of apt command upgrades all installed packages to latest level present on the configured repository

```
$ sudo apt upgrade
```

Get help

If you want help on usage of apt command you give help option

```
$ apt help
```

Search

search can be used to search for the given string in the list of available packages and display matches. You can also use this option, if you are looking for packages having a specific feature.

Syntax

```
$ sudo apt search keyword
```

Example

```
$ sudo apt search zip
```

Display information about the package

Syntax

```
sudo apt show package_name
```

Example

```
$ sudo apt show zip
Package: zip
Version: 3.0-11build1
Priority: optional
Section: utils
Origin: Ubuntu
Maintainer: Ubuntu Developers <ubuntu-devel-
discuss@lists.ubuntu.com>
Original-Maintainer: Santiago Vila <sanvila@debian.org>
Bugs: https://bugs.launchpad.net/ubuntu/+filebug
Installed-Size: 638 kB
Depends: libbz2-1.0, libc6 (>= 2.14)
Recommends: unzip
Homepage: http://www.info-zip.org/Zip.html
… (output truncated)
```

Clean

clean clears out the cache of apt which is kept locally

```
sudo apt clean
```

Difference between apt and apt-get

If you are coming from older version of Ubuntu or Debian, then you must be accustomed to apt-get command. You must be missing apt-get command. Good news is that, yes apt-get command still works but apt command provides more user friendly and provide more options for package management. apt consists some of the most widely used features from apt-get and apt-cache. Moreover, it can also manage apt.conf file. One of the key difference is the apt shows the progress bar while installing or removing a package. Other improvement is when you give apt update command it shows the number of packages that can be upgraded.

For the users who want to still want to use apt-get command here is the summary of commands. Please note all these command may require administrator access so whenever required use with sudo.

Function	Command
Install	apt-get install <packagename>
remove	apt-get remove <package_name>
Complete remove	apt-get purge <package_name>
Packages that were installed by other packages and no	apt-get autoremove

longer needed	

The apt-cache Command

If you want to use apt-cache instead of apt search command, Apt-cache can display much of the information stored in APT's internal database. This internal database is cache gathered for configured sources. This cache gets generated with apt update command.

Syntax

```
apt-cache search keyword
```

Example

```
$ sudo apt-cache search zip
```

dpkg

dpkg is a package manager for Debian-based systems. It is used to install locally available packages unlike apt you cannot download packages. With dpkg you can list, install, remove, and build packages.

List all installed packages

```
sudo dpkg -l
```

Display specific package

Syntax

```
sudo dpkg -l packagename
```

Example

```
$ sudo dpkg -l zip
```

```
adams@server1:~$ sudo dpkg -l zip
Desired=Unknown/Install/Remove/Purge/Hold
| Status=Not/Inst/Conf-files/Unpacked/halF-conf/Half-inst/trig-aWait/Trig-pend
|/ Err?=(none)/Reinst-required (Status,Err: uppercase=bad)
||/ Name                    Version              Architecture         Description
+++-=======================-====================-====================-========================================
ii  zip                     3.0-11build1         amd64                Archiver for .zip files
```

List the files installed by a package

Syntax

```
sudo dpkg -L <Package name>
```

Example

```
$ sudo dpkg -L zip
```

To see which package had installed the specific file

Syntax

```
dpkg -S <file name with path >
```

Example

```
$ sudo dpkg -S /etc/wgetrc
wget: /etc/wgetrc
```

Install a local package with .deb extension

Syntax

```
sudo dpkg -i <Package name>
```

Example

```
sudo dpkg -i zip_3.0-11_i386.deb
```

Remove package

Syntax

```
sudo dpkg -r <Package name>
```

Example

```
sudo dpkg -r zip
```

This will remove package from the system. Unlike **apt** it will not remove the dependent packages, so it is not recommended to uninstall packages using dpkg command.

Aptitude

Aptitude is text-based menu driven front-end to the APT. you can install remove and update packages with aptitude. As aptitude is menu driven it is easy to operate.

When you run aptitude you will see two pans top and button. Top pan contains categories like installed packages, Not installed packages and virtual packages etc. Bottom pan shows the detailed information related to packages. Let's first install aptitude if it is not there.

To install aptitude

```
$ sudo apt install aptitude
```

Following are example of how to do common package management tasks:

Install Packages

To install a package, press ENTER on **Not Installed Packages.** Under NOT installed there are categories. Select the category by pressing ENTER, suppose you want to install gargi font. After highlighting the required package with arrow keys, either press ENTER key or press + key to select for installation. Now press **g** two times to install package. After finishing press ENTER to return to aptitude or press **q** and ENTER to quite.

Remove Packages

To remove a package, locate the package under the Installed Packages package category, using arrow key and ENTER key highlight the package. Once highlighted press − key to mark the package for removal. Press g two times to remove the package.   After finishing press ENTER. Press **q** to return to main menu.

Update Package Index

To update the package index, press the **u** key.

Upgrade Packages

To upgrade packages, first update the package index and then press **U** key to mark all packages with updates. Now press **g** two times to download and upgrade the packages. After finishing press ENTER. Press **q** to return to main menu.

Command Line Aptitude

Aptitude can also use as command line like apt

Install package

Syntax

```
$ sudo aptitude install Package_name
```

Example

```
$ sudo aptitude install zip
```

Remove package

Syntax

```
$ sudo aptitude remove Package_name
```

Example

```
$ sudo aptitude remove zip
```

Repository

Repository is collection of software for Linux, ether present locally or remotely. The repository can be used to install additional software or to update the current software. The list of and location of repository can be either in /etc/apt/sources.list file or create file **/etc/apt/sources.list.d** directory. To add a repository add the entry in **/etc/apt/sources.list** it should be one source per line.

Example

```
$ cat /etc/apt/sources.list
deb http://archive.ubuntu.com/ubuntu bionic main
deb http://archive.ubuntu.com/ubuntu bionic-security main
deb http://archive.ubuntu.com/ubuntu bionic-updates main
```

/etc/apt/sources.list.d

To add the additional repositories you can create files in /etc/apt/sources.list.d directory. The format of files in /etc/apt/sources.list.d is same as **sources.list** file and the file names should end with **.list**.

Extra Repositories

There are some repositories like **Main** and **Restricted** which are officially supported by Ubuntu but you can also add additional repository for more packages these repositories are community maintained repositories. Two most popular are **Universe** and **Multiverse** repositories. Where **universe** is Community maintained software, i.e. not officially supported software. **Multiverse** repository often have software with licenses which prevent then to bundle with a free operating system.

PPA

A Personal Package Archive (PPA) is a special software repository. Mostly it is maintained by people who are not official Ubuntu developer. These are third party repositories. The prime example of third party repositories are google, Mythtv webupd8 etc.

To add PPA

On the command line you can add a PPA using add-apt-repository command

```
$ sudo add-apt-repository ppa:kubuntu-ci/unstable
```

After adding repository

```
$ sudo update
```

Creating local repository

In my 20 years of experience, I was not privileged to get internet on production Linux server most of the time due to security reasons. So if you are in my situation you are struck if you have to install additional software. At this situation local repository comes to your rescue. The steps to create local repository are bellow:-

1. Mount the Ubuntu server DVD

   ```
   mkdir /cdrom
   $ sudo mount /dev/cdrom /cdrom
   ```

2. Edit /etc/apt/sources.list file and add following entries.

   ```
   deb file:///cdrom bionic main restricted
   $ sudo apt update
   ```

apt.conf

apt.conf is main configuration used by apt located at /etc/apt/. it is not the only place you can configure apt, /etc/apt/apt.conf.d is another location where you can keep your apt configuration files. We usually use this apt.conf file to configure proxy for apt if your Ubuntu machine is behind internet proxy. To reach proxy server you either can create/edit **/etc/apt/apt.conf** file or can create a conf file under **/etc/apt/apt.conf.d** directory.

Configuring proxy for apt

First create apt.conf file at /etc/apt directory if it is not already there.

```
sudo vi /etc/apt/apt.conf
```

Add the following line to set your HTTP proxy

```
Acquire::http::Proxy "http://user:password@proxy.server:port/";
```

Example

```
Acquire::http::Proxy "http://10.10.10.1:8080";
```

If your proxy is HTTPS

```
Acquire::https::Proxy "https://10.10.10.1:8080";
```

/etc/apt/apt.conf.d /

If you like you can also place your apt configuration file in this directory. Create file with name like proxy.conf in /etc/apt/apt.conf.d/ directory

```
sudo vi /etc/apt/apt.conf.d/proxy.conf
```

Add the following line to set your HTTP proxy

```
Acquire::http::Proxy "http://user:password@proxy.server:port/";
```

Example

```
Acquire::http::Proxy "http://10.10.10.1:8080";
```

After creating this file you can verify also

```
$ sudo apt update
```

## Chapter 12

Backup and Restore

Data is very important part of computing. Computer viruses, hardware failures, user mistake, file corruption or natural disasters can cause data loss . Data loss can cost organization huge financial loss or customer loss. Taking regular backup can prevent this type of situation, as in case of any type of data loss you can easily restore it. There are many backup utilities and suites available on Ubuntu, Some are free others are paid. We will discuss few free utilities which you will find in almost all Linux and UNIX flavors.

Tar

Most common and widely used utility for Linux is Tar. Tar is used for creating one archive file of multiple files. This archive file can be kept as backup on tape or other media. You can also create compressed archive file by providing addition options with tar command.

Create tar

Syntax

```
tar cvf name_of_archive_file files_or_directory_to_archive
```

Where

c   create

v	verbose
f	Allows you to specify the filename of the archive

Example

In this example we will create achieve file abc.tar from all files in the current directory

```
$ sudo tar cvf abc.tar *
$ ls -la
total 96
drwxr-xr-x. 4 root root  4096 Feb 12 10:58 .
drwxr-xr-x. 3 root root  4096 Feb  4 12:46 ..
-rw-r--r--. 1 root root 81920 Feb 12 10:58 abc.tar
```

Create compressed tar file

Create gzip format tar file

To create gzip compression format file

Syntax

```
tar cvfz name_of_tarfile.tar.gz name_of_files_to_backup
```

Example

```
$ tar cvfz abc.tar.gz *.log
```

Create bzip format

To create bzip compression format file

Syntax

```
tar cvfj name_of_tarfile.tar.bz2 name_of_files_to_backup
```

```
$ tar cvfj abc.tar.bz2 *.log
```

Untar

Syntax

```
tar xvf name_of_archive_file
```

Where

x   extract

v   verbose

f   file name types of achieve file

Example

```
$ tar xvf abc.tar
```

Uncompressing

Uncompress gzip format

Syntax

```
tar xvfz filename
```

Example

```
$ tar xvfz abc.tar.gz
```

Uncompress bzip format

Syntax

```
tar xvfj filename
```

Example

```
$ tar xvfj abc.tar.bz2
```

List

To list the content of archive file

Syntax

```
tar tvf filename
```

Example

```
$ tar tvf abc.tar
```

List gzip compressed tar file

Syntax

```
tar tzvf filename
```

Example

```
$ tar tzvf abc.tar.gz
```

List bgzip compressed tar file

Syntax

```
tar tjvf filename
```

Example

```
$ tar tjvf abc.tar.bz2
```

CPIO

Another conventional utility for backup is cpio. Cpio is versatile utility for backup. This utility can also be used for creating and extracting achieve and to copy files from one place to another.

Create achieve

To create archive with cpio command we have to provide list of files to archive/ backup from another command

Syntax

```
Command |cpio -ov >output file
```

Example

In this example, we will use ls command to provide list of files in the current directory. This list will be used by cpio command to create achieve file abc.cpio.

```
$ cd abc
$ sudo ls |cpio -ov > /backup/abc.cpio
```

Extracting

Syntax

```
cpio -idv < archive file name
```

Example

In this example we will extract the archived file created in previous example to directory newbackup

```
$ mkdir newbackup
$ cd newbackup
$ sudo cpio -idv < /backup/abc.cpio
```

How to create archive list of specific files.

If you want to take backup of specific type of files or name you can use find command as list of files.

Syntax

```
find . -iname <pattern> |cpio -ov > output file
```

Example

In this example we will archive all log files present in the current directory and its sub directories.

```
$ find . -iname *.log -print|cpio -ov > /backup/selog.cpio
```

Using cpio to create tar file

In the previous section we explored the tar command you may be astonished to know that you can also use cpio command to create tar files as shown below:-

```
$ ls|cpio -ovH tar -F abc.tar
```

To extract tar file using cpio

```
$ cpio -idv -F abc.tar
```

These are few most common utilities for backup but if you are looking for automated backup solution, you can use shell scripts to take backup. You can also use other tools available on Linux like Bacula, rsync, timeshift, Amanda, Time Vault etc. For proprietary options that are more sophisticated, you can use EMC networker, IBM Spectrum Protect, Veeam etc.

## Chapter 13

Utilities and commands

In this chapter we will discuss some of the common command utilities very useful in Ubuntu administration. Most of the commands discussed in chapter can be used on almost any flavor of Linux.

cp

Command to copy files

Syntax

```
cp <options> source destination
```

Example

```
cp /home/abc.txt /home1/
```

Copy all files in the directory recursively

```
cp -R  /home/* /home1/
```

Prompt before any overwrite

```
cp -i /home /home1
```

Copy all new files to the destination

```
cp -u * /tmp
```

Forcefully copy files

```
cp -f /tmp/abc.txt /backup/.
```

Copy without prompting to overwrite

```
cp -n * t
```

scp

scp command is used to copy files from one host to another host in secured manner.

Copy files from local machine to remote machine

Syntax

```
scp filename remote_user@remote_host:/some/remote_diectory
```

Example

```
$ scp /home/ana/atom.txt adams@server1/home/adams/.
```

Copy files from remote host to local host

Syntax

```
scp remote_user@remote.host:/path/filename .
```

Example

```
$ scp adams@server1/home/adams/tasks.txt /home/ana/.
```

ls

Lists the names of Files

Syntax

`ls -<options>`

Example

`$ ls -al`   To list directories and files

cat

Displays a Text File

Syntax

`cat filename`

Example

`$ cat abc.conf`

rm

Deletes a file, files or directory

Syntax

`rm filename`

Example

`rm abc.conf`

To delete abc directory recursively

`rm -r abc`

more

When you want to view a file that is longer than one screen, you can more utility. More is used for paging through text one screen full at a time.

Syntax

```
more filename
```

Example

```
more /etc/hosts
```

less

Less is a program similar to more, but it allows backward movement in the file as well as forward movement.

Syntax

```
less filename
```

Example

```
less /etc/hosts
```

mv

mv command is used to move file from one location to other location. mv command can also be used to rename the file.

mv command to move file

Syntax

```
mv filename destination_directory
```

Example

```
mv a.txt /tmp/.
```

It will move a.txt file from current directory to /tmp directory

To rename

Syntax

```
mv filename newfilename
```

Example

```
mv a.txt b.txt
```

grep

Searches for a String from one or more files. Display each line which has string.

Syntax

```
grep string file
```

Example

```
grep '127.0.0.1' /etc/hosts
```

head

Print the first 10 lines of file to standard output. You can also specify how many line it will show.

Syntax
```
head option file
```

Example
```
head -20 /tmp/abc.txt
```
This command will show first 20 lines of abc.txt file

tail

Print the last 10 lines of file to standard output if used without any parameter, otherwise you can specify number of lines to display.

Syntax
```
tail option file
```

Example
```
tail -20 /var/log/logfile
```
It will show last 20 lines

Use tail to monitor file continuously

```
tail -f /var/log/logfile
```

It will show end of growing file. Press **Ctrl +c** to interrupt.

diff

Compares Two Files.

Syntax
```
diff First_file   Second_file
```

Example
```
diff abc.txt bbc.txt
```

file

Determine file type

Syntax
```
file file_name
```

Example
```
file bbc.txt
```

echo

Write arguments to the standard output

Syntax

echo text

Example

```
echo hello
```

date

Print or change the system data and time.

Syntax

```
date
```

Example

To check date

```
date
```

To set date

```
date -s "24 feb 2017 19:00"
```

Chapter 14

Piping and Redirection

In the previous chapter we learned Linux commands in this chapter we will see how Linux commands and files can be used in conjunction with one another to turn simple commands into much more complex command. This involves movement of data from command to other command or command to file or file to command.

This data traveling from command to other command or file to command or file to command is known as stream. Stream can of three types:-

- Standard input (stdin)
- Standard output (stdout)
- Standard error (stderr)

Normally when user is working on a PC, standard input flows from keyboard of the user to standard out that is the monitor, where user see the output. If there are errors in the operation the user will see the standard error on the terminal. However, we can change this behavior by using angle brackets and pipes. Some time we refer these streams with their corresponding numbers.

Stream	Number	Sign	Append
stdin	0	<	<<
stdout	1	>	>>
stderr	2	2>	2>>

Redirection

When you want change the normal flow of data we use redirection. You can send output of the command to file or device. You can also take input from file or device to command.

Sending output to file (>)

Normally, we get our output on the screen, but if we wish to save it into a file, then greater than operator (>) is used to send the standard out to file. Please note this command will overwrite content of the existing output file.

Syntax

```
Command > filename
```

Example

```
ls > abc.txt
```

Sending input from file (<)

If we use the less than operator (<) then we can read data from file and feed it into the program via it's STDIN stream.

Syntax

```
Command < filename
```

Example

```
wc -l < abc.txt
```

Sending standard error to file

If we use 2 with greater than operator (2>) then we can send STDERR stream to a file.

Syntax

```
Command or script 2> filename
```

Example

```
myscript 2>abc.log
```

Append

We have seen that use of the single-bracket command overwrites the prior contents of the file. To append the content we can use double brackets (>>) or (2>>)

To append the standard out to existing file or create new one if it is not there

Syntax

```
Command >> filename
```

Example

```
# la -la >> abc.txt
```

To append the stderr stream to file

Syntax

```
Command 2>> filename
```

Example

```
# myscript.sh 2>> abc.txt
```

Sometimes, you might want to redirect both standard output and standard error into same file. This is often done in case of automated processes so that you can review the output and errors if any, later. Use &> or &>> to redirect both standard output and standard error to the same place. Another way is to use the numbers of the stream 2>&1

Syntax

```
Command >outputfile 2>&1
```

Example

```
ls b* >abc.log 2>&1
```

Piping (|)

For sending data from one program to another we use pipe
(|)

Syntax

Command1 | Command2

Example

```
ls | head -10
```

This command run the ls command and shows only first 10 lines of the output. This is simple example of pipe to explain, but you can use pipe for more complex use.

First sort the abc.txt and then use uniq command print unique values.

```
$ sort abc.txt | uniq
```

## Chapter 15

Compression utilities

Compression is process to reduce the size of a file by using different algorithms and mathematical calculations. Compression is very useful as it saves disk space. To save the backup files or to transfer files from one system to other compression is used. Compression only reduces the file size but if you want to create single from multiple files achieving is there. Gzip and bzip2 are compression tools only whereas zip can do both compression and archiving, there are three most utilities to compress the files

Compression	Extension	Uncompress
bzip2	bz2	bunzip2
gzip	gz	gunzip
zip	zip	unzip

Compress

Bzip2 format

bzip2 is a file compression program that uses the Burrows–Wheeler algorithm. It only compresses single files and is not a file archiver. Each file is replaced by a compressed version of itself, with the same name plus bz2 extension (original_name.bz2). Each compressed file has the same file permissions and modification time as the original file. When you decompress it, these properties get correctly restored.

Syntax

```
bzip2 file_to_compress
```

Example

```
root@server1:~# ls -la abc.nlt
-rw-r--r-- 1 root root 74 Sep 18 04:46 abc.nlt
root@server1:~# bzip2 abc.nlt
root@server1:~# ls -la abc.nlt*
-rw-r--r-- 1 root root 98 Sep 18 04:46 abc.nlt.bz2
```

bunzip2

To decompress the file which had been compressed with bzip2 command use bunzip2 utility

Syntax

```
bunzip2 compressed_file_name
```

Example

```
root@server1:~# bunzip2 abc.nlt.bz2
root@server1:~# ls -la abc.nlt*
-rw-r--r-- 1 root root 74 Sep 18 04:46 abc.nlt
root@server1:~#
```

In this example date of modification of file remain same.

gzip format

gzip is a file compression program that uses the DEFLATE algorithm. It only provide compression of single files and is not a file archiver. Each single file is compressed into a single file with **gz** added extension. The compressed file consists of a GNU zip header and deflated data. Like bzip2 each compressed file has the same file permissions, and, modification time as the original file. When you decompress it these properties get correctly restored.

Syntax

```
gzip file_to_backups
```

Example

```
root@server1:~# ls -la abc.nlt
-rw-r--r-- 1 root root 74 Sep 18 04:46 abc.nlt
root@server1:~# gzip abc.nlt
root@server1:~# ls -la abc.nlt*
-rw-r--r-- 1 root root 95 Sep 18 04:46 abc.nlt.gz
```

gunzip

To decompress the file compressed with gzip utility you require gunzip utility

```
root@server1:~# gunzip abc.nlt.gz
root@server1:~# ls -la abc.nlt*
-rw-r--r-- 1 root root 74 Sep 18 04:46 abc.nlt
```

zip format

zip is file compression archive utility. Zip not only compress the file but can put two more compressed files in to one file along with its information. Unlike gzip and bzip it will not replace the original file.

Syntax

```
zip zipfile.zip file_to_compress
```

Example

```
root@server1:~# zip xyz.zip abc.*
  adding: abc.log (stored 0%)
  adding: abc.nlt (deflated 7%)
  adding: abc.txt (deflated 62%)
root@server1:~# ls -l
total 16
-rw-r--r-- 1 root root  50 Sep 18 04:42 abc.log
-rw-r--r-- 1 root root  74 Sep 18 04:46 abc.nlt
-rw-r--r-- 1 root root 661 Sep 18 03:41 abc.txt
-rw-r--r-- 1 root root 816 Sep 18 06:54 xyz.zip
```

unzip

unzip is the utility to decompress

Syntax

```
unzip compressed_file
```

Example

```
root@server1:~# mkdir test
root@server1:~# mv xyz.zip test
root@server1:~# cd test
root@server1:~/test# unzip xyz.zip
Archive:  xyz.zip
 extracting: abc.log
  inflating: abc.nlt
  inflating: abc.txt
root@server1:~/test# ls -l
total 16
-rw-r--r-- 1 root root  50 Sep 18 04:42 abc.log
-rw-r--r-- 1 root root  74 Sep 18 04:46 abc.nlt
-rw-r--r-- 1 root root 661 Sep 18 03:41 abc.txt
-rw-r--r-- 1 root root 816 Sep 18 06:54 xyz.zip
```

## Chapter 16

Managing services

Daemons

Daemons are processes, which run in the background and not interactively. Daemons perform some predefined actions at predefined time. Generally, daemons start at bootup and remain till shutdown. Mostly daemons name ends with **d**.

Services

Earlier versions of Linux there used be scripts located in the /etc/rc.d/init.d/ directory used to control state of service and daemons.

In recent versions, these init scripts have been replaced with service units, service units reside in **/etc/systemd/system/** directory. Service units end with the .service file extension. **systemctl** command is used to view, start, stop, restart, enable, or disable system services.

Service can start at boot time using **systemctl enable name.service** command

Service Status Management

Detail	Command
Starts a service	systemctl start name.service Example systemctl start iscsi.service
Stops a service	systemctl stop name.service Example systemctl stop iscsi.service
Restarts a service	systemctl restart name.service Example systemctl restart iscsi.service
Restarts a service only if it is running.	systemctl try-restart name.service Example systemctl try-restart iscsi.service
Reloads configuration	systemctl reload *name*.service Example systemctl reload iscsi.service
Checks if a service is running.	systemctl status *name*.service or systemctl is-active *name*.service Example systemctl status iscsi.service
Displays the status of all service	systemctl list-units --type service --all or systemctl -at service

Enable and disable service at startup

Detail	Command
Enable service	systemctl enable *name*.service Example systemctl enable iscsi.service
Disable service	systemctl disable *name*.service Example systemctl disable iscsi.service
To prevent service from starting dynamically or even manually unless unmasked	systemctl mask *name*.service Example systemctl mask iscsi.service
Check whether a service enabled or not	systemctl is-enabled *name*.service Example systemctl is-enabled iscsi.service
Lists all services and checks if they are enabled or not	systemctl list-unit-files --type service

Service unit information

When we give command **systemctl -status name.service**. It provides following information

Field Description

Field	Description
Loaded	Whether the service unit is loaded, the absolute path to the unit file, whether the unit is enabled.
Active	Running or not
Main PID	PID of the service
Process	Information about process
CGroup	Information about Control Groups.

Example

$sudo systemctl status nfs-kernel-server.service

● nfs-server.service - NFS server and services

   Loaded: **loaded** (/lib/systemd/system/nfs-server.service; enabled; vendor preset: enabled)

   Active: **active** (exited) since Sun 2017-04-09 17:43:46 IST; 1h 2min ago

   Process: 1410 ExecStart=/usr/sbin/rpc.nfsd $RPCNFSDARGS (code=exited, status=0/SUCCESS)

   Process: 1401 ExecStartPre=/usr/sbin/exportfs -r (code=exited, status=0/SUCCESS)

   Main PID: 1410 (code=exited, status=0/SUCCESS)

    Tasks: 0

   Memory: 0B

     CPU: 0

   CGroup: /system.slice/nfs-server.service

.. output truncated ….

systemd Targets

Previous versions of Ubuntu implemented run level. Run level is state or mode of OS in which it will run. Each run level causes certain number of services to be stopped or started providing control over behavior of machine. This has been replaced by **systemd targets** there were seven **Runlevels** replaced by corresponding **target units**

Run level	Description	Target unit
0	halt the machine	poweroff.target
1	single user mode	rescue.target
2	multiuser with command line no GUI	multiuser.target
3	multiuser with command line no GUI	multiuser.target
4	multiuser with command line no GUI	multiuser.target
5	multiuser with GUI	graphical.target
6	reboot	reboot.target

Commands

List currently loaded target

```
systemctl list-units --type target
```

Change the target

Switch to multiuser

```
systemctl isolate multi-user.target
```

Switch to GUI mode

```
systemctl isolate graphical.target
```

Change default target

```
systemctl set-default <name of target>.target
```

Viewing the Default Target

```
systemctl get-default
```

Changing the Current Target

```
systemctl isolate <name of target>.target
```

Managing services startup

To list all services and there status

```
systemctl -at service
```

To list current setting of specific service

Syntax

```
systemctl status name.service
```

Example

```
systemctl status httpd.service
```

Enabling service

Syntax

```
systemctl enable name.service
```

Example

```
systemctl enable iscsi.service
```

To disable service

Syntax

```
systemctl disable name.service
```

Example

```
systemctl disable iscsi.service
```

Managing the services status

Determine status of service

Syntax

```
systemctl status name.service
```

Example

```
systemctl status httpdd.service
```

Starting service

Syntax

```
systemctl start name.service
```

Example

```
systemctl start httpd.service
```

Stopping service

Syntax

```
systemctl stop name.service
```

Example

```
systemctl stop httpd.service
```

Restarting service

Syntax

```
systemctl restart name.service
```

Example

```
systemctl restart httpd.service
```

Install new service

Procedure to install new service

Install new service package

```
$ sudo apt install service_name
```

Configure the service to start automatically at startup

```
$ sudo systemctl enable name.service
```

Start the service

```
$ sudo systemctl start name.service
```

Example

```
$ sudo apt install vsftpd
$ sudo systemctl enable vsftpd
$sudo systemctl start vsftpd
```

## Chapter 17

SSH

SSH provides a secure channel over unsecure network in a client server architecture. SSH is a replacement of telnet, which is a insecure protocol. It allows secure channel to login and execute command securely because all communication between client and server is encrypted.

Ssh command format

```
ssh -x user@hostname
```

Whenever ssh connection is made to system first time the public key of remote system is stored locally so it's identity can be verified next time.

If you are connecting from MS windows client to Linux server, you require third party software like **putty**. Use **CTRL + d** key or exit command will terminate **ssh** session.

ssh key

ssh keys helps in identifying yourself to a server using public key cryptography and challenge response authentication. ssh keys are generated in pair one public and private key. The public is for sharing and private key is for you. It must be kept safely.

Server having public key can send challenge, which can only be answered by server holding private key. This allows password less login.

Passwordless login

In this example we will configure password less login to **server2** from **server1**

1. Create keys on **server1** host

```
server1 ~]$ ssh-keygen
```

2. Copy public key from **server1** to **server2**

```
$ scp ~/.ssh/id_rsa.pub user1@server2:/home/user1/id_rsa.server1.pub
```

3. On **server2** create directory .ssh in the home directory of the user and change its permissions.

```
server2 ~]$ mkdir .ssh
server2 ~]$chmod 700 .ssh
```

4. Append the public key file to **authorized_keys** file and change permissions.

```
server2~]$ cat id_rsa.server1.pub >> .ssh/authorized_keys
```

```
server2 ~]$ chmod 644 .ssh/authorized_keys
```

5. Now try login from server one i.e **server1** to **server2** it
   should not ask for password.

```
server1 ~]$ ssh user1@server2
```

## Chapter 18

FTP

FTP is file transfer protocol. It is used for transfer of files between the computers on the network. It is based on client server model.

Server

As ftp works on client server model, you have wide range of chooses for ftp server on Ubuntu, **vsftp** (very secure FTP) server is one of popular FTP server available on Ubuntu. It is very easy to install and configure, so lets start and deploy vsftp .

Deploying vsftp

Install the package

```
sudo apt install vsftpd
```

Start the server

```
systemctl start vsftpd
```

Enable the service to start at startup

```
systemctl enable vsftpd
```

Access to an FTP server can be in two ways:

1. Authenticated
2. Anonymous

Authenticated

By default, access to FTP server is configured as Authenticated. Users can connect to ftp server using their credentials. User are allowed to download files only. If you want to enable users to upload files also edit /etc/vsftpd.conf file

```
write_enable = YES
```

Now reload the configuration vsftpd:

```
sudo systemctl reload vsftpd
```

Anonymous

You can connect to ftp server anonymously also. it allows you to download files from **/srv/files/ftp** directory anonymously.   By default, vsftpd is not configured for anonymous download. To enable anonymous download edit /etc/vsftpd.conf and change

```
anonymous_enable=Yes
```

Make Directory for ftp users

```
sudo mkdir /srv/files/ftp
sudo usermod -d /srv/files/ftp ftp
```

After making the change, reload the configuration of vsftpd:

```
sudo systemctl reload vsftpd.service
```

FTP clients are used for desktops, servers, and mobile devices. Few decades ago, FTP clients were just command line interface (CLI) applications. However, over the time it has developed and FTP client is available in mainly in three type

1. GUI
2. Web browser
3. Command line

Command Line FTP

As this book emphasize on command line we will see how we will use command FTP client to connect to FTP server to upload and download files.

Syntax

```
ftp < server IP address or hostname >
```

It will ask for username and password use Linux username and password for server. If anonymous is enabled you can give ftp or anonymous as username and email address as password.

To upload file on ftp prompt

```
sftp> put file_name
```

To download file

```
sftp> get file_name
```

To exit

```
sftp> bye
```

Example

```
~]$ ftp server1
Connecting to server1...
User1@server1's password:
ftp> pwd
Remote working directory: /home/user1
ftp> cd /etc/
ftp> pwd
Remote working directory: /etc
ftp> get hosts
Fetching /etc/hosts to hosts
/etc/hosts
100%    84      0.1KB/s    00:00
ftp> bye
```

## Chapter 19

Web server

A webserver is program, which allows web browser clients to access web pages. It uses HTTP (Hypertext Transfer Protocol). Apache is the most popular web server on the internet, it is used to serve more than half of all active websites. Apache HTTP server is also avaialble on Ubuntu.

Deploying http server

Install http server

```
$ sudo apt install apache2
```

Start service

```
$ sudo systemctl start apache2.service
```

Default directory where http keeps contents

/var/www/html

Configuration file

Configuration files of Apache is located in /etc/apache2 directory.

apache2.conf this is the main configuration file for the server. Almost all configuration can be done within this file.

Test

1. Create file in directory /var/www/html/index.html and Write **Hello**
2. Save the file and exit
3. Open the firefox on the address bar write http://<server Ip address>
4. You should see hello

Virtual Hosts

The Apache HTTP Server offers option to create multiple websites on single webserver using virtual hosts. Based on host name, IP address or port number, virtual hosts allows same webserver to provide different information. With name-based virtual hosting, you can host multiple websites on a single machine with a same IP address. Virtual hosting is suitable for shared web hosting environments, where multiple websites are hosted on a single server or VPS.

Steps to host multiple sites on single server using virtual hosting:-

1. Create the directory structure
2. Create web pages for each host
3. Set ownership and permissions

4. Configure your virtual host directories

5. Change the Apache configuration file

6. Create virtual host configuration files

7. Verify the configuration files and restart the apache2 service

8. Create DNS record in /etc/hosts file or on the DNS server

9. Test the virtual hosts

Steps in detail

In this example, we will host two websites abcexample.com and xyzexample.com on same IP Address.

Create Directory Structure

First, create directory for each website to hold html files. This directory is known as document root for each website

```
$ sudo mkdir -p /var/www/html/abcexample.com
$ sudo mkdir -p /var/www/html/xyzexample.com
```

Create web pages for each host

```
$ sudo vi /var/www/html/abcexample.com/index.html
```
Add following content

```
Abcexample.com
```
Save the file and exit from vi

Same way

```
# vi /var/www/html/xyzexample.com/index.html
```

Add following content

```
Xyzexample.com
```

Save the file and exit from vi

Set ownership and permissions

Set the ownership of newly created directories to apache user and group using chown with sudo. You can check the user and group in /etc/apache2/envvars. For Ubuntu default user and group is www-data

```
chown -R www-data:www-data /var/www/html/abcexample.com
chown -R www-data:www-data /var/www/html/xyzexample.com
```

Change the /var/www/html folder readable by world

```
$ sudo chmod -R 755 /var/www/html
```

Create virtual host configuration files

Create configuration files for each virtual host

```
$ sudo vi /etc/apache2/sites-available/abcexample.com.conf
```

```
<VirtualHost *:80>
    ServerName www.abcexample.com
    ServerAlias abcexample.com
    DocumentRoot /var/www/html/abcexample.com
</VirtualHost>
```

```
$ sudo vi /etc/apache2/sites-available/xyzexample.com.conf
```

```
<VirtualHost *:80>
    ServerName www.xyzexample.com
    ServerAlias xyzexample.com
    DocumentRoot /var/www/html/xyzexample.com
</VirtualHost>
```

Create soft links of virtual host configuration files in **sites-enabled** directory (Note this command is in single line, due to page width limitation it is wrapped to next line. When you issue this command issue it in single line)

```
$ sudo ln -s /etc/apache2/sites-available/abcexample.com.conf
/etc/apache2/sites-enabled/abcexample.com.conf
```

Or you can give command

```
$ sudo a2ensite abcexample.com.conf
```

```
$ sudo ln -s /etc/apache2/sites-available/xyzexample.com.conf
/etc/apache2/sites-enabled/xyzexample.com.conf
```
or
```
$ sudo a2ensite xyzexample.com.conf
```

Verify the configuration files and restart the httpd service

Verify the configuration files

```
$ sudo apachectl configtest
```

135

Restart Service

```
# sudo systemctl reload apache2.service
```

Create DNS record in /etc/hosts file or in the DNS server

If you have DNS server you can add the entries for

www.abcexample.com

www.xyzexample.com

For testing purpose you can add the entries in /etc/hosts

```
vi /etc/hosts
192.168.131.152   www.abcexample.com
192.168.131.152   www.zyzexample.com
```

Test the new websites (virtual hosts)

Open your web browser on Server in GUI Mode and go to the URLs

http://www.abcexample.com

and

http://www.xyzexample.com.

You will see the content of each website

## Chapter 20

Squid

A proxy server is a server that acts as an intermediary between the server and client. Proxies can perform many added-value functions to enhance the overall user experience. Squid is full featured cache proxy server providing proxy and caching services for HTTP, HTTPS, FTP, and other protocols. Squid offers access control, authorization and logging environment for web proxy and content serving applications. It also provides cache for DNS lookup.

Installation

First install the squid application using apt command

```
$ sudo apt-get install squid
```

Squid.conf is main configuration file of squid. To be on safe side make a copy of the /etc/squid/squid.conf so that in case you mess up while editing you have at least original one as a starting point.

```
$ sudo cp /etc/squid/squid.conf /etc/squid/squid.conf.org
```

Edit the /etc/squid/squid.conf

```
$ sudo vi /etc/squid/squid.conf
```

For basic configuration and demonstration purpose look for following directive in the file

http_port : This is the default port for the HTTP proxy server, by default it is 3128, you may change it to any other port that you want, like http_port 8888.

visible hostname : hostname of squid. For example prox1

http_access deny all : This line will block access the HTTP proxy server access, you need to change it to http_access allow all to start using your Squid proxy server.

Once you made required changes restart the squid service.

```
$ sudo systemctl restart squid.service
```

On the client configure your browser to use this server as proxy with configured port. Suppose IP Address of quid machine is 192.168.1.10 and port configured as 8888 then add this IP and port for proxy server settings on the client.

Logs

Default logs for squid are in **/var/log/squid**. You may check **/var/log/squid/access.log** file if you faced any errors or if you want to see which websites are being visited by people using Squid proxy server.

## Chapter 21

NFS Network File System

Network File System (NFS) is file sharing file system, which works on server and client model. Developed by Sun microsystem it is widely used as shared file system on Linux and Unix machines. NFS (Network File System) allows you to share a directory located on one computer with other computers on the network. The computer where directory located is known as server and computers, which is mounting/using this shared directory, are known as client. User on clients uses this shared directory by mounting on local mount point. Over the period, NFS has gone under tremendous improvements therefore came up with different versions. The different versions of NFS are: -

1. NFS V1
2. NFS V2
3. NFS V3
4. NFS V4

Where NFS V3 and NFS V4 are more recent version of NFS, V3 is safer and asynchronous works on UDP protocol while V4 has added advantage of working through firewall and works on TCP.

Installation

NFS server

First check if NFS server package is already installed

```
$ dpkg -l | grep nfs-kernel-server
```

Now install the packages

```
$ sudo apt-get install nfs-kernel-server
```

Start the service

```
$ sudo systemctl start nfs-kernel-server.service
```

Exporting NFS directories

Once package is installed now we have to export directories (Shared Directories which will be available on the client). For that we will use **/etc/exports** file. /etc/export is a configuration file used for exporting file system located on server to clients.

Edit **/etc/exports** file and add the file systems you want to export.

```
$ sudo vi /etc/exports
```

The format of the files is like that:-

```
mountpoint    [host][permissions/options]
```

where

mountpoint mount point of the file system (directories) to export

host the IP address or hostname of the client you want give access of the file systems. You can also put * if you want to give access to all clients.

Permissions/Options it can be **ro** for read only, **rw** for read write, with **sync** option changes are written before replying next request.

Example

```
/cdrom server2(rw,sync,no_subtree_check)
```

To export the file systems after adding in the exports files.

```
$ sudo exportfs -a
```

On the client

Install the required packages:

```
$ sudo apt-get install nfs-common
```

On the client check the file systems exported by server

Syntax

```
$ showmount -e server IP address / hostname
```

Example

```
$ sudo showmount -e server1
```

Mount the exported file system

```
$ sudo mount -t nfs server1:/userfs /newmnt
```

Where

-t for type of filesystem

server1 is hostname of the server

/userfs is exported directory

/newmnt is local mount point (directory) on which the remote file system will be mounted

Export filesystem temporarily

```
$ sudo exportfs -i *:/mnt
```

Verify

```
$ sudo showmount -e
/mnt *
```

Commands to manage NFS server

Check if service is running or not

```
$ sudo systemctl status nfs-kernel-server
```

Start the service

```
$ sudo systemctl start nfs-kernel-server
```

Stop the service

```
$ sudo systemctl stop nfs-kernel-server
```

If NFS server is not starting automatically at boot

```
$ sudo systemctl enable nfs-kernel-server
```

Disable NFS automatic start

```
$ sudo systemctl disable nfs-kernel-server
```

To unexport all exported file system

```
$ sudo exportfs -ua
```

## Chapter 22

Time Synchronization

It is very important to keep the time of the server to be accurate. When your servers are in production environment it is ideal to keep all servers time in sync. Whenever there is problem in any of the server to correlate the problem with other server the time stamp in the log file is very important. Ubuntu 18.04 has time synchronization built in and activated by default using **system-timesyncd** service it replaces old NTP services. In this chapter we will learn configuration and management of time synchronization services in Ubuntu.

Configuration file

The main configuration files for timesyncd is /etc/systemd/timesyncd.conf

The default file is like that

```
[Time]
#NTP=
#FallbackNTP=ntp.ubuntu.com
#RootDistanceMaxSec=5
#PollIntervalMinSec=32
#PollIntervalMaxSec=2048
```

Steps to configure timesyncd

You can check the current status of time and time configuration using two command timesyncd and timedatctl

Using timedatectl

`$ timedatectl status`

Local time: Thu 2018-09-13 03:08:53 UTC

Universal time: Thu 2018-09-13 03:08:53 UTC

RTC time: Thu 2018-09-13 03:08:53

Time zone: Etc/UTC (UTC, +0000)

System clock synchronized: yes

systemd-timesyncd.service active: yes

RTC in local TZ: no

This command shows time and status of timesyncd

Verify the status using timesyscd service

`$ sudo systemctl status systemd-timesyncd`

• systemd-timesyncd.service - Network Time Synchronization

  Loaded: **loaded** (/lib/systemd/system/systemd-timesyncd.service; enabled; vendor preset: enabled)

  Active: **active** (running) since Thu 2018-09-13 02:02:40 UTC; 1h 8min ago

    Docs: man:systemd-timesyncd.service(8)

 Main PID: 642 (systemd-timesyn)

   Status: "Synchronized to time server 91.189.89.198:123 (ntp.ubuntu.com)."

   Tasks: 2 (limit: 1082)

  CGroup: /system.slice/systemd-timesyncd.service

          └─642 /lib/systemd/systemd-timesyncd

This command shows the status of the service and the external ntp server it is using to synchronize.

If you want to change to different server or you have local ntp server you want to use you can change the /etc/systemd/timesyncd.conf .

Edit /etc/systemd/timesyncd.conf to add the external server to sync by uncommenting NTP and add the NTP server hostname or IP address.

```
[Time]
NTP=0.in.pool.ntp.org
#FallbackNTP=ntp.ubuntu.com
#RootDistanceMaxSec=5
#PollIntervalMinSec=32
#PollIntervalMaxSec=2048
```

Restart the systemd-timesyncd service and verify the status

```
$ sudo systemctl restart systemd-timesyncd
$ sudo  systemctl status systemd-timesyncd
● systemd-timesyncd.service - Network Time Synchronization
   Loaded: loaded (/lib/systemd/system/systemd-
timesyncd.service; enabled; vendor preset: enabled)
   Active: active (running) since Thu 2018-09-13 03:11:55 UTC;
4s ago
     Docs: man:systemd-timesyncd.service(8)
 Main PID: 3649 (systemd-timesyn)
   Status: "Synchronized to time server 123.108.200.124:123
(0.in.pool.ntp.org)."
```

```
        Tasks: 2 (limit: 1082)
       CGroup: /system.slice/systemd-timesyncd.service
              └─3649 /lib/systemd/systemd-timesyncd
```

timedatectl

The timedatectl command allows you to query and change the configuration of the system clock and its settings. In this section we will explore some of the common use of this command

Check the current timezone

Syntax

```
timedatectl
```

Example

```
$ timedatectl
                      Local time: Fri 2018-09-14 04:02:13 UTC
                  Universal time: Fri 2018-09-14 04:02:13 UTC
                        RTC time: Fri 2018-09-14 04:02:13
                       Time zone: Etc/UTC (UTC, +0000)
       System clock synchronized: no
systemd-timesyncd.service active: yes
                 RTC in local TZ: no
```

OR

Syntax

```
timedatectl | grep Time
```

Example

```
$ timedatectl | grep Time
                       Time zone: Etc/UTC (UTC, +0000)
```

147

To view all available timezones

Syntax

```
timedatectl list-timezones
```

Filter the output for specific region

```
timedatectl list-timezones | egrep -o "America/N.*"
```

Set local timezone

Syntax

```
timedatectl set-timezone new_timezone
```

Example

```
adams@server1:~$ sudo timedatectl set-timezone Asia/Tokyo
adams@server1:~$ timedatectl | grep Time
                Time zone: Asia/Tokyo (JST, +0900)
```

It is recommended to set the time zone to UTC

Syntax

```
timedatectl set-timezone UTC
```

Example

```
$ sudo timedatectl set-timezone UTC
$ timedatectl | grep Time
                Time zone: UTC (UTC, +0000)
```

148

To set the time if automatic time synchronization is disabled

Syntax

```
timedatectl set-time <newtime>
```

Example

```
$ sudo timedatectl set-time 09:15
```

To set the date use the same command with date format YYYY-MM-DD

Syntax

```
timedatectl set-time <new date>
```

Example

```
$ sudo timedatectl set-time 2018-09-20
$ timedatectl
              Local time: Thu 2018-09-20 00:00:02 UTC
          Universal time: Thu 2018-09-20 00:00:02 UTC
                RTC time: Thu 2018-09-20 00:00:03
               Time zone: UTC (UTC, +0000)
 System clock synchronized: no
systemd-timesyncd.service active: no
             RTC in local TZ: no
```

Set the date and time simultaneously

Syntax

```
timedatectl set-time '201809-20 09:15:50'
```

Example

```
$ sudo timedatectl set-time '2018-09-20 09:15:50'
$ timedatectl
                  Local time: Thu 2018-09-20 09:15:55 UTC
              Universal time: Thu 2018-09-20 09:15:55 UTC
                    RTC time: Thu 2018-09-20 09:15:55
                   Time zone: UTC (UTC, +0000)
     System clock synchronized: no
systemd-timesyncd.service active: no
               RTC in local TZ: no
```

A Linux system actually has two clocks: One is the battery powered **Real Time Clock** and other is **System clock**. Real Time Clock (RTC) also referred as CMOS clock or "Hardware clock" keeps track of time when the system is turned off. RTCs often provide alarms and other interrupts. RTC is not used when the system is running. When system boots System clock takeover the control. System Clock is a software clock maintained by the kernel. It does not exist when the system is not running. Software clock or Kernel clock get initialized from the RTC or some other time source at boot time. So at boot time the system clock will often be set to the current clock time using an RTC.

To set the hardware clock

Set your hardware clock to local time zone. This command will give warning also.

Syntax

150

timedatectl set-local-rtc 1

```
$ sudo timedatectl set-local-rtc 1
[sudo] password for adams:
$ timedatectl
                  Local time: Thu 2018-09-20 09:35:37 UTC
              Universal time: Thu 2018-09-20 09:35:37 UTC
                    RTC time: Thu 2018-09-20 09:35:37
                   Time zone: UTC (UTC, +0000)
   System clock synchronized: no
systemd-timesyncd.service active: no
             RTC in local TZ: yes
```

Warning: The system is configured to read the RTC time in the local time zone.This mode can not be fully supported. It will create various problems with time zone changes and daylight saving time adjustments. The RTC time is never updated, it relies on external facilities to maintain it. If at all possible, use RTC in UTC by calling 'timedatectl set-local-rtc 0'.

Set your hardware clock to sync with UTC

```
$ sudo timedatectl set-local-rtc 0
$ timedatectl
                  Local time: Thu 2018-09-20 09:41:07 UTC
              Universal time: Thu 2018-09-20 09:41:07 UTC
                    RTC time: Thu 2018-09-20 09:41:07
                   Time zone: UTC (UTC, +0000)
   System clock synchronized: no
systemd-timesyncd.service active: no
             RTC in local TZ: no
```

Use NTP server

To Use remote NTP server (private or public), type the following command at the terminal.

Syntax

```
# timedatectl set-ntp true
```

Example

```
$ sudo timedatectl set-ntp true
```

```
$ sudo timedatectl set-ntp true
adams@server1:~$ timedatectl
                    Local time: Thu 2018-09-20 09:46:04 UTC
                Universal time: Thu 2018-09-20 09:46:04 UTC
                      RTC time: Thu 2018-09-20 09:46:06
                     Time zone: UTC (UTC, +0000)
     System clock synchronized: no
systemd-timesyncd.service active: yes
               RTC in local TZ: no
```

To disable NTP time synchronization

Syntax

```
# timedatectl set-ntp false
```

Example

```
$ sudo timedatectl set-ntp false
$ timedatectl
                      Local time: Thu 2018-09-20 09:50:20 UTC
                  Universal time: Thu 2018-09-20 09:50:20 UTC
                        RTC time: Thu 2018-09-20 09:50:22
                       Time zone: UTC (UTC, +0000)
     System clock synchronized: no
systemd-timesyncd.service active: no
                 RTC in local TZ: no
```

## Chapter 23

Firewall

According to dictionary, a firewall is a wall or partition designed to inhibit or prevent the spread of fire. In computer world, firewall is network security system used to secure the incoming and outgoing connections. It prevents unauthorized access to the system. It restricts user to access only designated services and ports.

Netfilter is framework provided by the Linux kernel which allows various networking functions like packet filtering, Network Address Translation and port translation. Firewall uses netfilter for port filtering. Iptables is userspace interface for managing kernel's packet filtering system. The main function of IPtable is to handover the packet to netfilter whenever packet reaches to the server. You can manage the firewall using iptables. However, to make your life more simple there many frontends are available to manage the firewall rules. Ubuntu provides **ufw** (uncomplicated firewall) as frontend for configuration of IP4 and IP6 host-based firewall. ufw is by default disabled to enable it

Enable Firewall

```
$ sudo ufw enable
```

Disable Firewall

```
$ sudo ufw disable
```

View current configuration of firewall

```
$ sudo ufw status
```

Detailed status of firewall

```
$ sudo ufw status verbose
```

Port based configuration

Open Specific port

Syntax

```
$ sudo ufw allow port_no
```

Example

```
$ sudo ufw allow 22
```

Close Specific port

Syntax

```
$ sudo ufw deny port_no
```

Example

```
$ sudo ufw deny 22
```

To remove specific rule

Syntax

```
$ sudo ufw delete rule
```

Example

```
$ sudo ufw delete deny 22
```

Allow ssh from specific hosts

Syntax

```
$ sudo ufw allow proto tcp from hostname to any port
```

Example

```
$ sudo ufw allow proto tcp from 192.168.0.1 to any port 22
```

Allow all ssh from specific network

Syntax

```
$ sudo ufw allow proto tcp from network to any port
```

Example

```
$ sudo ufw allow proto tcp from 192.168.0.0/24 to any port 22
```

Application based Configuration

Instead of configuring ports we can also use application profile to configure the firewall. The configuration based on application profile is much easy, just give the application name it will automatically allow or deny the required ports and protocols. **ufw** application profile contains information of ports and protocols needed by application to function properly. These profiles are kept in **/etc/ufw/applications.d** directory. You can edit the configuration if required.

View installed application profiles

```
$ sudo ufw app list
```

Allow app

Syntax

```
$ sudo ufw allow app
```

Example

```
$ sudo ufw allow Apache
```

Show port configuration of an application profile

Syntax

```
sudo ufw app info application
```

Example

```
sudo ufw app info Apache
```

Allow traffic from specific network to application

```
sudo ufw allow from 192.168.0.0/24 to any app Apache
```

IP Masquerade

IP Masquerade, also called IPMASQ or MASQ. It allows one or more computers in a network with private, non-routable assigned IP addresses to communicate with the Internet using the Linux server doing masquerading. The server doing masquerading acts as a gateway and all the devices using masquerading are invisible behind it. For other machines on internet the traffic appears to be coming from the IPMASQ server and not from the machines behind the IPMASQ. To do this, the kernel modifies the source IP address of each packet. To track source machine of connection Linux uses Connection Tracking (conntrack).

In Ubuntu you can masquerade the connection using either ufw or iptables

IP masquerading using iptables

Edit **/etc/sysctl.conf** and uncomment this line
```
net.ipv4.ip_forward=1
```

now execute the new configuration
```
$ sudo sysctl -p
```

Now add the IP table rule

```
$ sudo iptables -t nat -A POSTROUTING -s 192.168.1.0/24 -o
ens33 -j MASQUERADE
```

Description of the command options

-t nat   type of rule is NAT

-A POSTROUTING -A for appending to the POSTROUTING chain

-s 192.168.1.0/24 the rule applies to traffic originating from the specified address space in this case 192.168.1.0

-o ens33 Interface name

-j MASQUERADE   traffic matching this rule is to jump to the MASQUERADE target

Masquerading using ufw

First edit **/etc/default/ufw** and change the line
`DEFAULT_FORWARD_POLICY="DROP"`
To
`DEFAULT_FORWARD_POLICY="ACCEPT"`

Like in iptables section edit **/etc/sysctl.conf** and uncomment this line
`net.ipv4.ip_forward=1`

now execute the new configuration
```
$ sudo sysctl -p
```

Now add rules to the **/etc/ufw/before.rules** file

nat table rules

*nat

:POSTROUTING ACCEPT [0:0]

Forward traffic from ens31 through ens33.

-A POSTROUTING -s 192.168.1.0/24 -o ens33 -j MASQUERADE

don't delete the 'COMMIT' line or these nat rules won't be
processed(For each Table a corresponding COMMIT statement is
required.)

COMMIT

Finally apply the changes to ufw by disable and enable
commands

$ sudo ufw disable

$ sudo ufw enable

Logs

Once your firewall is working now it's time to monitor it.
Firewall can be monitored by it logs. First you have to enable
the logging of ufw

$ sudo ufw logging on

Once logging is enabled you check logs in
/var/log/syslog, /var/log/kern.log and
/var/log/messages files

160

## Chapter 24

Partition and file system

Partitions

Partition is to divide the storage, mostly hard disk into segments in which you can have more than one filesystem. These file systems can be of same or different type. Partitioning of storage helps in managing storage properly. Many tools are available in Ubuntu for partitioning the disk. Ubuntu **fdisk** is one of the widely used tool for partitioning.

To list the partition table

```
$ sudo fdisk -l
```

List the partition table for specific disk

Syntax

```
fdisk -l <device name >
```

Example

```
$ sudo fdisk -l /dev/sda1
```

Create new partition on device

In this example /dev/sda2 is added to system

1. First check the new device added

```
$ sudo fdisk -l
Disk /dev/sdb: 21.5 GB, 21474836480 bytes
255 heads, 63 sectors/track, 2610 cylinders
Units = cylinders of 16065 * 512 = 8225280 bytes
Sector size (logical/physical): 512 bytes / 512 bytes
```

it will show the all storage device

2. Run fdisk on required device

```
fdisk /dev/sdb
```

3. Print partition table of the selected disk

Press **p** and **enter** key

```
Command (m for help): p

Disk /dev/sdb: 21.5 GB, 21474836480 bytes
255 heads, 63 sectors/track, 2610 cylinders, total 41943040
sectors
Units = sectors of 1 * 512 = 512 bytes
Sector size (logical/physical): 512 bytes / 512 bytes
I/O size (minimum/optimal): 512 bytes / 512 bytes
Disk identifier: 0xdec2ee90
   Device Boot      Start         End      Blocks   Id  System
```

4. Press **n** for new partition
5. Press **p** for primary
6. Give partition number like **1, 2, 3, 4**
7. Press **Enter** for starting section
8. For last sector, give size like +1G to create 1 GB partition

```
Command (m for help): n
Command action
   e   extended
   p   primary partition (1-4)
p
Partition number (1-4): 1
First sector (2048-41943039, default 2048):
Using default value 2048
Last sector, +sectors or +size{K,M,G} (2048-41943039, default
41943039): +1G
```

9. Press **w** to write on disk

Filesystem

File System is method used by operating system to store data and retrieve it. File system helps in managing and arranging data. The difference between a disk or partition and the filesystem it contains is important. Although you can access the partition which we created in the previous section directly using as raw device, but most of the programs uses disk or partition using another layer which is known as Filesystem. Over the time many type filesystem were developed each filesystem has its own pro and cons. Few of most popular filesystems available on Linux specially on Ubuntu are EXT, XFS, ZFS, JFS etc.

163

EXT File System

Extended file system (EXT) is most popular file system used in Linux Operating systems. In its lifespan it had evolved a lot from its first implementation in 1992 to till date. EXT 4 is the most recent version of EXT. From third generation i.e. **EXT 3** it came up with journalized file system. With JFS feature it keep the track of changes not yet committed to the file system by recording such changes in data structure to journal which in turn generate circular log. In case of abrupt system down like power failure or crashed file system can be brought back online easily. **EXT3** having limitation of file system size as 8TB /16TB and file size as 2 TB whereas **Ext4** is the next generation of ext file system having improved file system and file size upper limits of 16TB. It is efficient reliable and robust. Ext4 is a deeper improvement over Ext3.

Creating EXT file system

1. Create partition using fdisk.
2. **fdisk -l** check the device name.
3. **mkfs -t ext4 /dev/sdb1** where **sdb1** is device name and **ext4** is file system type.

```
$ sudo mkfs -t ext4 /dev/sdb1
```

4. create mount point

```
$ sudo mkdir /test1
```

5. **Add entry in the /etc/fstab**

```
$ sudo vi /etc/fstab
```

```
/dev/mapper/server1--vg-swap_1 none    swap      sw      0        0
/dev/sdb1         /test1   ext4      defaults 0 2
```

Where**/dev/sdb1** is device **/test1** mount point, **ext4** for partition type, 0 for dump and 2 order for fsck.

6. Mount the file system

```
$ sudo mount -a
```

Mounting DVD automatically after reboot

1. Make directory for mounting

```
$ sudo mkdir /cdrom
```

2. edit the /etc/fstab file

```
$ sudo vi /etc/fstab
```

3. Add following line

```
/dev/cdrom        /cdrom              iso9660 ro           0 0
```

4. Mount and check if it is mounted

```
$ sudo mount -a
$ df -hT
```

## Chapter 25

Swap space

Swap space is used in Linux and UNIX to free up physical memory. The inactive pages of data are written to slower storage i.e. hard disk. The area where inactive data is written is known as swap space. Swap space can be a dedicated swap partition, a swap file, or a combination of swap partitions and swap files. If you do automatic partition, it will create swap file instead of swap file system. Although Ubuntu supports swap file however it is recommended to have dedicated swap partition.

Swap should be double or more the size of physical RAM if RAM is up to 2 GB. If Physical RAM is more than 2 GB then swap space should be equal to the size of Physical RAM. In any case it should not less than 32 MB.

Add swap space

1. Create partition

```
$ sudo fdisk /dev/sdb

Command (m for help): n
Command action
   e   extended
```

```
    p   primary partition (1-4)
p
Partition number (1-4): 2
First cylinder (307-6132, default 307):
Using default value 307
Last cylinder, +cylinders or +size{K,M,G} (307-6132, default
6132): +500M
```

2. Change the type by pressing **t** of partition selected to **82** which is **Linux swap**

```
Command (m for help): t
Partition number (1-4): 2
Hex code (type L to list codes): 82
Changed system type of partition 2 to 82 (Linux swap /
Solaris)
```

3. Check the partition

```
Command (m for help): p

Disk /dev/sdb: 21.5 GB, 21474836480 bytes
171 heads, 40 sectors/track, 6132 cylinders
Units = cylinders of 6840 * 512 = 3502080 bytes
Sector size (logical/physical): 512 bytes / 512 bytes
I/O size (minimum/optimal): 512 bytes / 512 bytes
Disk identifier: 0xdec2ee90

Device Boot    Start    End     Blocks   Id  System
/dev/sdb1       2048  2099199  2097152   1G  83 Linux
/dev/sdb2    2099200  3123199  1024000   500M 82 Linux swap / Solaris
```

4. Press w to write partition to disk

```
Command (m for help): w
The partition table has been altered!
```

5. **mkswap /dev/sdb2** where sdb2 is name of the partition which will be used as swap.

```
$ sudo mkswap /dev/sdb2
Setting up swap space version 1, size = 500 MiB (524283904
bytes)
no label, UUID=a1f34d13-7ab8-4f1e-ac6f-32b8c68e87e
```

6. Add entry in /etc/fstab

```
$ sudo cat /etc/fstab
```

```
/dev/sdb1          /test1  ext4      defaults 0 2
UUID=1f34d13-..6f-32b8c68e87e swap swap     defaults 0 0
```

7. **swapon -a** will activate swap

8. swapon -s will show status of all swap space

```
$ sudo swapon -s
```

Filename	Type	Size	Used	Priority
/dev/dm-1	partition	2097148	0	-1
/dev/sdb2	partition	511996	0	-2

To deactivate the swap space

```
$ sudo swapoff /dev/sdb2
```

File as swap space .

Create directory

```
$ sudo mkdir /swap
```

Create file with **fallocate** or **dd** of required size, in this example we are creating 2GB file.

```
$ sudo fallocate -l 2G /swap/first.swap
```

or.

```
sudo dd if=/dev/zero of=/swap/first.swap bs=1024 count=2097152
```

Format the file for swap.

```
$ sudo mkswap /swap/first.swap
```

Add this line to the end of /etc/fstab

```
/swap/first.swap swap swap    defaults 0 0
```

Activate swap file

```
$ sudo swapon /swap/first.swap
```

Check all Swap space

```
$ sudo swapon -s
```

Filename	Type	Size	Used	Priority
/swap.img	file	1970172	0	-2
/swap/first.swap	file	2097148	0	-3

Chapter 26

Logical Volume Manager

In earlier section we learned how to create partition as Linux filesystem but we can also create partition type as LVM (logical partition manager). When we create LVM type partition, LVM manages space allocated to it. Which is more sophisticated than normal Linux partition. LVM has following benefits

- Grow the filesystem dynamically
- Shrink the filesystem
- Add disk dynamically
- Mirroring
- Stripping
- Snapshot as backup of File system

Terms used in LVM

Physical Volume

Physical Volume (PV) is physical storage unit of an LVM is a block device such as a partition or whole disk. To use the device for an LVM create partition with **fdisk** as **LVM** type.

Volume Groups

One or more than one physical volumes combined to create Volume Group (VG).

Physical Extent

Storage space from Physical Volume is divided in to small unit of fixed size known as physical extent, which is smallest unit that can be allocated. P.E. will be same for all physical volume in the same VG.

Logical extent

Each logical volume is further divided into chunks of data, known as logical extents. Mapping of PE to LE make up front end of LVM. By default, one PE is mapped to one LE but, you can map more than one PE to one LE in case of mirroring.

Logical Volume

Logical volume is group of Logical Extent. It is here we create File system. Logical volume is not restricted to physical disk sizes. In addition, the hardware storage layer is isolated from software.

How to Create FS on newly added disk

1. Create Physical volume (PV)
   Use **fdisk** command and create partition type Linux LVM **8e**

```
$ sudo fdisk /dev/sdb

WARNING: DOS-compatible mode is deprecated. It's strongly recommended to
         switch off the mode (command 'c') and change display units to
```

```
              sectors (command 'u').
Command (m for help): n

Command action
    e   extended
    p   primary partition (1-4)
p
Partition number (1-4): 3
First cylinder (615-6132, default 615):
Using default value 615
Last cylinder, +cylinders or +size{K,M,G} (615-6132, default 6132):
+5G


Command (m for help): t
Partition number (1-4): 3
Hex code (type L to list codes): 8e
Changed system type of partition 3 to 8e (Linux LVM)


Command (m for help): p


Disk /dev/sdb: 21.5 GB, 21474836480 bytes
171 heads, 40 sectors/track, 6132 cylinders
Units = cylinders of 6840 * 512 = 3502080 bytes
Sector size (logical/physical): 512 bytes / 512 bytes
I/O size (minimum/optimal): 512 bytes / 512 bytes
Disk identifier: 0xdec2ee90


   Device Boot      Start         End      Blocks   Id  System
/dev/sdb1               1         307     1048576   83  Linux
/dev/sdb2             307         614     1050280   82  Linux swap /
Solaris
/dev/sdb3             615        2148     5246280   8e  Linux LVM


Command (m for help): w
```

```
The partition table has been altered!
```

2. Reboot the server

3. Create PV using command **pvcreate** *device_name* where *device_name* is device created with fdisk

```
$ sudo pvcreate /dev/sdb3
   Physical volume "/dev/sdb3" successfully created
$ sudo pvdisplay /dev/sdb3
   "/dev/sdb3" is a new physical volume of "5.00 GiB"
   --- NEW Physical volume ---
   PV Name              /dev/sdb3
   VG Name
   PV Size              5.00 GiB
   Allocatable          NO
   PE Size              0
   Total PE             0
   Free PE              0
   Allocated PE         0
   PV UUID              EQ7ElZ-WiGK-Z0m5-5gSN-gP95-MFSk-pKyTvS
```

4. Create Volume Group (VG)
   vgcreate *VG_name PV_name*

```
$ sudo vgcreate vg01 /dev/sdb3
   Volume group "vg01" successfully created
```

5. Create new Logical Volume(LV)
   lvcreate -n *LV_name* -L *size VG_name*

```
$sudo lvcreate -n lv01 -L 1G vg01
```

174

```
Logical volume "lv01" created
```

6. Create Filesystem on LV
   mkfs -t ext4 /dev/*VG_name*/*LV_name*

```
$ sudo mkfs -t ext4 /dev/vg01/lv01
```

7. Check the UUID of newly created file system

```
$ sudo blkid /dev/vg01/lv01
```

8. Create directory to mount

```
$ sudo mkdir /newfs
```

9. Add entry to **/etc/fstab** to mount filesystem automatically at startup

```
UUID=6acaa-5541..e830e  /newfs    ext4    defaults      1 2
```

10. Mount the file system

```
mount -a
```

Physical Volume Commands

Description	Command
Display PV properties	pvdisplay
Show all LVM block devices	pvscan

Prevent allocation of PE on PV	pvchange-xn */dev/PV_name*
Remove PV	pvremove */dev/PV_name*

Volume Group Commands

Description	Command
Display VG properties	vgdisplay
Display VG List	vgs
Add PV to VG	vgextend vgname */dev/PV_name* **Example** vgextend vg01 /dev/sdb5
Remove PV from VG	vgreduce vg1 */dev/PV_name* **Example** vgreduce vg01 /dev/sdb5
Activating VG	vgchange -ay *VG_name*
Deactivating VG	vgchange -ay *VG_name*
Remove VG	vgremove *VG_name* **Example** vgremove /dev/vg02
Create the special files for volume group devices	vgmknodes

Moving Volume group from one system to other

1. On first system where VG is currently running unmount all FS which is part of VG

```
$ sudo umount /newfs
```

2. Deactivate the VG **vgchange –an *VG_name*** command

```
$ sudo vgchange -an sharedvg
```

3. Export the VG with **vgexport *VG_name*** command

```
$ sudo vgexport sharedvg
```

4. After attaching HDD to new system import the VG with **vgimport *VG_name*** command

```
$ sudo vgimport sharedvg
```

5. Activate the VG with **vgchange -ay VG_name**

```
$ sudo vgchange -ay sharedvg
```

6. Mount the file systems on the VG

```
$ sudo mount /dev/sharedvg/sharedlv /mnt
```

7. Check the contents of file system

```
$ cd /mnt
$ ls
```

Extending FileSystem

1. Check the current FS size
   df -h /fsname

```
/dev/mapper/vg01-lv01        1008M   34M  924M   4%  /newfs
```

2. Check if you have enough free space i.e. free PE on the VG where LV of FS you want extend is there.

```
$ sudo vgdisplay vg01
  --- Volume group ---
  VG Name               vg01
  System ID
  Format                lvm2
  Metadata Areas        1
  Metadata Sequence No  5
  VG Access             read/write
  VG Status             resizable
  MAX LV                0
  Cur LV                1
  Open LV               1
  Max PV                0
  Cur PV                1
  Act PV                1
  VG Size               5.00 GiB
  PE Size               4.00 MiB
  Total PE              1280
  Alloc PE / Size       256 / 1.00 GiB
  Free  PE / Size       1024 / 4.00 GiB
  VG UUID               EXKfhW-MfE4-4ZtU-uQuM-v9e4-AJ9k-Uo6z4B
```

179

3. Extend the Logical Volume **lvextend -L size /dev/vgname/lvname**

```
$ sudo lvextend -L +200M /dev/vg01/lv01
  Extending logical volume lv01 to 1.20 GiB
  Logical volume lv01 successfully resized
```

4. Extend the filesystem using **resize2fs -p /dev/vgname/lvname**

```
$ sudo resize2fs -p /dev/vg01/lv01
```

5. Check the FS size **df -h /fsname**

```
/dev/mapper/vg01-lv01          1.2G    34M    1.1G    3%  /newfs
```

Reduce the Filesystem

1. Check the current FS size **df -h /fs_name**

```
/dev/mapper/vg01-lv01          1.2G    34M    1.1G    3%  /newfs
```

2. unmount the Filesystem **umount /fs_name**

```
$ sudo umount /newfs
```

3. Check the file system

```
$ sudo e2fsck -f /dev/mapper/vg01-lv01
```

4. Resize FS
   resize2fs -p /dev/vgname/lvname size

$ sudo resize2fs -p /dev/mapper/vg01-lv01 1G

In this example make the size of FS as 1 GB

5. Now reduce the LV size keep some extra space than filesystem
   lvreduce -L size /dev/vgname/lvname

$ sudo lvreduce   -L 1.1G /dev/mapper/vg01-lv01

6. Mount File system
   mount /fs_name

$ sudo mount /newfs

☐

181

## Chapter 27

LVM snapshot

LVM snapshot is a point in time copy of Logical Volume. The snapshot provides static view of original volume. Once snapshot has been taken we can use this snapshot to take backup volume, as snapshot is static copy and it will not change while backup is happening unlike the original volume which is dynamic.

The snapshot volume size should be enough to store the data that will change after snapshot has been taken. The volume will store only changes after the snapshot has been taken.

Create snapshot LV

1. Check the LV name and size of File System for which you want to create snapshot

```
$ sudo df -hT /newfs
Filesystem          Type  Size  Used Avail Use% Mounted on
/dev/mapper/vg01-lv01 ext4 1008M   34M  924M   4% /newfs
```

2. Check you have space at least equivalent to 10% of file system you want to take snapshot available on the VG where original LV is located

```
$ sudo vgdisplay vg01
```

3. Create LV 8 to 10 % of capacity of original LV
   lvcreate -s -n snaplvname -L size /dev/vgname/orginal_lv_name

```
$ sudo lvcreate -s -n snaplv1 -L 100M /dev/mapper/vg01-lv01
```

4. if you want to see content of snapshot LV
   mount -o ro /dev/vgname/snaplv /mount_point_snaplv

```
$ sudo mount -o ro /dev/vg01/snaplv1 /snapfs/
```

5. Change to directory to check the contents
   cd /mount_point_snaplv

```
$cd /snapfs/
$ls
```

Remove snapshot LV

1. Unmount snap File system
   umount /mount_point_snaplv

```
$ sudo umount /snapfs
```

2. Remove the snap logical
   lvremove /dev/vgname/snaplv

```
$ sudo lvremove /dev/mapper/vg01-snaplv1
```

Chapter 28

Identify your system

As an administrator, it is good practice to document the configuration and settings of your server. Proper documentation of server saves your time and time of the other people who are using the server. Following are the few commands to know your server.

Know the installed version of Ubuntu

```
$cat /etc/lsb-release
```

Know running kernel version

```
$ uname -r
```

or

```
$ cat /proc/version
```

Display CPU information

```
$ lscpu
```

or

```
$ cat /proc/cpuinfo
```

List all PCI devices

```
$ lspci
```

Detailed description of system hardware

```
$ sudo dmidecode
```

Display memory information

```
$ cat /proc/meminfo
```

or

```
$ free -m          shows memory in MB
```

List block device

```
$ sudo lsblk
```

List all partitions

```
$ sudo fdisk -l
```

List CPU, Memory, Process

```
$ sudo top
```

Display Hostname

```
$ hostname
```

## Chapter 29

System Monitoring Tools

Continues monitoring is vital part of the system administration. System monitoring helps in properly provision resources for your projects. It also helps in fine tuning the server. Monitoring helps in avoiding the unnecessary down time due to resource bottleneck as proper monitoring you can add the required hardware before it leads to server crash or denial of service. Sometime monitoring helps in predicting the hardware failure for example you can use smart tools to predict hard disk failure.

Viewing system processes

ps

Display report of running process. It is a snapshot of the current processes at time of running command.

To see every process on the system and their owner

ps aux

To list all related threads after each process

ps axms

Top

top command displays processor activity of Linux machine The top command displays list of running processes on the system It also displays additional information about current usage of CPU, memory and swap space.

```
$ sudo top
```

```
top - 21:59:05 up  5:58,   3 users,   load average: 0.16, 0.03, 0.01
Tasks: 188 total,   1 running, 187 sleeping,   0 stopped,   0 zombie
%Cpu(s):  0.0 us,  0.7 sy,  0.0 ni, 97.7 id,  1.0 wa,  0.3 hi,  0.3 si,  0.0
st
KiB Mem :  2045748 total,   168512 free,  1038120 used,   839116 buff/cache
KiB Swap:  2097148 total,  1906704 free,   190444 used.   891936 avail Mem

    PID USER      PR  NI    VIRT    RES    SHR S %CPU %MEM     TIME+ COMMAND
   1771 root      20   0  406112  10888   7084 S  0.3  0.5   0:30.40 vmtoolsd
   5854 root      20   0  156652   3960   3456 R  0.3  0.2   0:00.03 top
      1 root      20   0  215220   8316   5820 S  0.0  0.4   0:09.58 systemd
      2 root      20   0       0      0      0 S  0.0  0.0   0:00.03 kthreadd
      3 root      20   0       0      0      0 S  0.0  0.0   0:02.07
ksoftirqd/0
      5 root       0 -20       0      0      0 S  0.0  0.0   0:00.00
kworker/0:0H
      7 root      20   0       0      0      0 S  0.0  0.0   0:01.05 rcu_sched
      8 root      20   0       0      0      0 S  0.0  0.0   0:00.00 rcu_bh
      9 root      20   0       0      0      0 S  0.0  0.0   0:01.07 rcuos/0
     10 root      20   0       0      0      0 S  0.0  0.0   0:00.00 rcuob/0
     11 root      rt   0       0      0      0 S  0.0  0.0   0:00.00
migration/0
     12 root       0 -20       0      0      0 S  0.0  0.0   0:00.00 lru-add-
drain
.. output truncated
```

Free

Free command provides information about system memory and swap space

```
$ sudo free
        total     used       free     shared  buff/cache    available
Mem:   2045748  1066888    135120   7596       843740        863048
Swap:  2097148   193704   1903444
```

To view memory in Megabytes

```
$ sudo free -m
```

lsblk

The **lsblk** command displays information about available block devices, which includes block device's major and minor number, size, type and mount point.

```
$ sudo lsblk -a
```

blkid

To get UUID of a block device

```
$ blkid /dev/sda1
/dev/sda1: UUID="b4bd566c-8591-4695-a55f-28335f914a11" TYPE="ext4"
PARTUUID="f2acf7d4-01"
```

Partx

The **partx** command display a list of disk partitions.

```
$ sudo partx -s /dev/sda
NR    START        END   SECTORS  SIZE NAME UUID
 1     2048    2099199   2097152   1G        f2acf7d4-01
 2  2099200   41943039  39843840  19G        f2acf7d4-02
```

findmnt

The **findmnt** command allows you to list all mounted filesystems

```
$ sudo findmnt
```

du

The **du** command allows you to display disk usage by files in a directory

```
$ du
4          ./Templates
4          ./Music
4          ./.pki/nssdb
8          ./.pki
24         ./.gnupg
```

To display output in human readable format i.e. the size in KB and MB

```
$ du -h
4.0K    ./Templates
4.0K    ./Music
... Output truncated ..
```

Display summary

```
$ du -sh
```

df

The **df** command displays report of file system disk space usage.

To display the disk space usage by each file system

```
$ df -h
Filesystem            Size  Used Avail Use% Mounted on
devtmpfs              476M     0  476M   0% /dev
tmpfs                 487M  336K  487M   1% /dev/shm
tmpfs                 487M  2.4M  485M   1% /run
```

www.ingramcontent.com/pod-product-compliance
Lightning Source LLC
Chambersburg PA
CBHW031239050326
40690CB00007B/867